The HOLLYWOOD CANTEEN

WHERE THE GREATEST GENERATION DANCED WITH THE MOST BEAUTIFUL GIRLS IN THE WORLD

BY LISA MITCHELL AND BRUCE TORRENCE
WITH A FOREWORD BY JOAN LESLIE

The Hollywood Canteen: Where the Greatest Generation Danced With the Most Beautiful Girls in the World
© 2012 Lisa Mitchell and Bruce Torrence. All Rights Reserved.

No part of this book may be reproduced in any form or by any means, electronic, mechanical, digital, photocopying or recording, except for the inclusion in a review, without permission in writing from the publisher.

Published in the USA by:
BearManor Media
PO Box 1129
Duncan, Oklahoma 73534-1129
www.bearmanormedia.com

ISBN 978-1-59393-409-5

Printed in the United States of America.
Book design by Brian Pearce | Red Jacket Press.

To Terry Richey
In gratitude for his loving encouragement and solidarity.

And to Bruce Torrence who made this project so much fun.
— L.M.

Ditto to L.M.
And to all the volunteers who generously gave their time and talent to make the Hollywood Canteen a success.
— B.T.

TABLE OF CONTENTS

FOREWORD 9

PREFACE: THE HOME FRONT 11

THE HEART OF THE MATTER: HOW IT BEGAN 12

HOORAY FOR HOLLYWOOD 14

BUILDING A DREAM.. 18

FRIENDS IN HIGH PLACES 28

"ALL OF HOLLYWOOD IS YOUR HOST" 32

DAY IN, NIGHT OUT 40

RULES OF THE GAME 54

"WHAT STARS WILL BE HERE TONIGHT?" 64

"MISS HAYWORTH, MAY I HAVE THIS DANCE?" 86

A GOOD TIME FOR ALL: AN INTEGRATED CANTEEN............... 98

THE GREATEST SHOW IN TOWN.. 108

SPECIAL ATTRACTIONS 128

A PLACE TO STAY: THE HOLLYWOOD GUILD AND CANTEEN 150

CANTEEN ON THE SCREEN 158

"WE'LL MEET AGAIN..." CLOSING THE CANTEEN 174

EPILOGUE 181

APPENDIX 185

CHAPTER NOTES 197

SOURCES 201

ACKNOWLEDGEMENTS 203

INDEX 205

The people we have mentioned on the following pages are, by no means, the only ones who appeared at the Hollywood Canteen. For all of the thousands of volunteers — famous and unknown — that we have not been able to include, we sincerely apologize.

Joan Leslie rarely missed volunteering every Tuesday night.

FOREWORD

There's a little spot on a side street in Hollywood where magic used to happen every night during World War II. A plain old barn-like cafe was turned into a glamorous star-studded nightclub — a welcoming place for every soldier, sailor and Marine on furlough. And, along with her right hand man, John Garfield, Bette Davis made it happen. With her fabulous drive, she persuaded all the studio executives to support it and to promise that their stars would appear there regularly. She also cajoled the guild and union memberships to transform the old barn into an entertainment center that was like their own clubhouse. It was Hollywood's very own Canteen.

Tuesday night was Warner Brothers' night, and my dad always drove me over to the Canteen directly from the studio when shooting was over for the day. He dropped me off at the stage door entrance on Cole Place, where I would be checked in by the Officer of the Day (OD).

Once it was Hoagy Carmichael, who gave me a bear hug that I'll never forget. I would be assigned to handing out bologna and cheese sandwiches, coffee and cake that the servicemen wolfed down. Then I would sit at a table with a group of boys and ask about their hometowns and families, while they would ask me what it was like to kiss Gary Cooper! I would sign autographs on menus, caps, snapshots, shirts, dollar bills — whatever they gave me. I danced with the boys, too — sometimes with disastrous results to my elaborate hairdos!

And the shows! The crowd went wild when Marlene Dietrich would take the mike, when Bob Hope took over the stage to deliver one of his fabulous monologues. Bing Crosby would perform with his sons. I remember one Christmas show when the "Crosby Quartet" sang Christmas carols that the boys requested. All the big bands of the day made an appearance. Betty Hutton and the Andrews Sisters belted out popular songs over jitterbugging soldiers. Those guys were the most appreciative audience a performer could ever wish for!

When I remember the Canteen, most of all, I remember the faces of the servicemen: young men, thrilled at this glimpse of Hollywood glamour, deliriously happy on liberty, and yet willing to be sent out the next day to the other side of the world. When I think about those boys, so willing to fight for our country's honor, and of what they did for us, how could we not do our best for them? We may have stayed to close up for the night, but every volunteer's heart in the Hollywood Canteen went out the door with those men. I'm so proud I was a part of it.

Joan Leslie

PREFACE: THE HOME FRONT

"Although the treacherous attack on Pearl Harbor was the immediate cause of our entry into the war, that event found the American people spiritually prepared for war on a world-wide scale...

"Not all of us can have the privilege of fighting our enemies in distant parts of the world...

"But there is one battle where everyone in the United States — every man, woman, and child — is in action, and will be privileged to remain in action, throughout this war. That front is right here at home in our daily lives, and in our daily tasks."

President Franklin Delano Roosevelt
Fireside Chat, April 28, 1942

World War II opened a new chapter in the lives of depression-weary Americans. As husbands and fathers, sons and brothers shipped out to fight in Europe and the Pacific, citizens who remained at home were galvanized in support of a common goal: to actively maintain the home front. Millions of women marched into factories, offices, and military bases to work in the paying jobs formerly held by men in peacetime.

One of the greatest contributors to the war effort was Hollywood's entertainment industry; no other single group gave so much of its time, talent, energy, and enthusiasm. Hollywood film and radio stars, movie and studio employees, actors and actresses of varying degrees of fame, as well as screenwriters, directors, and producers, rolled up their sleeves to sell war bonds, traveled far and wide to perform for troops, and cheered up wounded servicemen on hospital tours.

But if there was one operation in which all the celebrated elements of Hollywood's wartime generosity met, it was the Hollywood Canteen.

For three years, the best nightclub in the world welcomed over three million servicemen to a unique haven in a converted stable-cum-playhouse in the heart of Hollywood. It was a magical combination of a dazzling glamour spot and a comfy home away from home.

Under its western-style roof, young men in uniform away from their families for the first time and about to ship out — some never to return — could actually dance with Betty Grable! They could laugh at Bob Hope, tell their troubles to motherly character actress, Beulah Bondi, be handed a sandwich by Rita Hayworth, and have a letter to their girl written by a sympathetic studio secretary.

Most of all, as the boys went off to face unseen dangers in unknown lands, they knew, beyond a shadow of a doubt, how much they were appreciated. They left the Hollywood Canteen armed with the kinds of hope and encouragement that would help them win a war.

CHAPTER 1

THE HEART OF THE MATTER: HOW IT BEGAN

It was the first full year of America at war, and 1942 found the country dancing to "Chattanooga Choo-Choo," listening to a new radio mystery called *Suspense*, and watching Walt Disney's *Bambi* and *Donald Gets Drafted* in movie theatres. It brought shortages of metal and leather, and rationing of coffee, sugar, and gasoline.

But there was no shortage of fervor among Americans for supporting the war in any way that they could. From school children to their grandparents, through Victory Gardens and scrap metal drives, war aid flourished everywhere. One remarkable expression of solidarity that became famous all over the world began over lunch one day by two citizens of Hollywood.

Two-time Academy Award winner Bette Davis was a respected artist, recognized as "the American screen's most accomplished actress."[1] She was also the quintessential movie star. Among the many classic films in which she lit up the screen, *Now, Voyager* (1942) is particularly memorable. It's such a *Bette* picture, full of dramatic physical and emotional transformations. Certainly it has one of the most romantic final scenes in all of movies. "Shall we just have a cigarette on it?" Paul Henreid says to Davis, agreeing to try to maintain their special territory of love. He puts two cigarettes in his mouth, lights them both, hands one to Davis. When he expresses his hope for their happiness, she replies, "Oh, Jerry, don't let's ask for the moon. We have the stars!" Max Steiner's music swells as the camera pans up through an open window to a shot of sparkling stars in the night sky. Fade Out. The End.

But as much of an asset as *Now, Voyager* was for Davis' career, it was something that went on behind the scenes that would lead to her greatest personal achievement. For it was while making *Voyager* at Warner Bros. in May, 1942, that Davis had lunch with John Garfield in the Green Room of the studio commissary.

John Garfield, who was from the New York stage, had been nominated for an Oscar as a supporting actor in his first picture — Warners' *Four Daughters* (1938). His naturalistic style of acting and brash, rebellious image would propel him to stardom in such intense films as *The Postman Always Rings Twice* (1946), *Humoresque* (1946), and *Body and Soul* (1947).

Though by 1942, Garfield was on track professionally with over a dozen films to his credit, a major goal eluded him: to serve his country at war. A childhood bout with rheumatic fever had left him with a weak heart, rendering him 4-F — unfit for military duty. Fortunately, he channeled his frustration into a constructive action that would benefit millions. Impressed by the work of the Stage Door Canteen in New York City, Garfield saw the need for a similar — yet unique to Hollywood — enterprise on the West Coast.

The Stage Door Canteen opened on March 4, 1942, three months after the United States entered the war against the axis of Japan, Germany and Italy. Started by the American Theater Wing, it was located just off Broadway in the basement of the 44th Street Theater, whose owner, Lee Shubert, donated its use. Stage designers created the interior décor, while local merchants, caterers, and restaurateurs provided food and beverages.

Up to 1700 volunteers from New York's theatrical industry offered their time as performers and service staff to keep this night club/soup kitchen open — even during blackouts and curfews. As many as 3,000 servicemen came to the Stage Door Canteen each night to sing, dance, eat, and be entertained.

When John Garfield sat down for that commissary lunch with Bette Davis, he told her about what he had seen in New York — and of his strong belief that Hollywood must have its own Canteen as soon as possible. There they were in the entertainment capitol of the world in a time of war. They had all the best ingredients right at their fingertips to give the boys something they'd never forget.

As Garfield outlined his concept of a Canteen to be run solely by members of Hollywood's considerable show business community, Davis caught his excitement. When he asked her to become the Canteen's chairman, she accepted with the vibrant determination for which she was known.

CHAPTER 2
HOORAY FOR HOLLYWOOD

Jimmy Ritz serves Coca Cola to Juanita Stark, Virginia Field, Jane Wyman and Air Cadets during the Canteen's fund-raising benefit at Ciro's.

Davis and Garfield flung themselves into the rigorous process of turning their dream into a reality. They spent weekends and eighteen-hour work days, as well as Sundays — their one day off from the studio — attacking the mountain of details involved in opening the Canteen.

One of their first tasks was to enlist the support of every guild, union, and craft organization affiliated with Hollywood's entertainment industry. They were met with a grand show of confidence as forty-two guilds and unions unanimously agreed to sponsor the endeavor; later the number would increase to forty-six.

In early June, Bette and John called for a meeting of several people who were committed to getting the Canteen off and running. They began by appointing a Board of Directors and electing a slate of officers. The Board members would be selected from representatives of the forty-two guilds and unions. The first roll of officers included Bette Davis, President; John Garfield, Carroll Hollister, and J.K. Spike Wallace, Vice Presidents; Alfred Ybarra, Treasurer; and Jean Lewin, Secretary. Over the years of the Canteen's existence, other people would be elected and appointed to the Board of Directors; various officers would include Mervin LeRoy, Mary Ford, Cay Baldwin, and Carey Wilson.

Shortly after being elected president, Bette Davis decided to ask Jules Stein to get involved with the Canteen. Stein, a former opthalmologist, was the founder and head of the Music Corporation of America (MCA), which represented Bette as her theatrical agency. Her personal agent at MCA was Lew Wasserman, who had been groomed by Stein as a booking agent. Even though she had been with MCA for three years, she had never actually met Jules Stein. In fact, not many people in Hollywood knew Stein; few even knew what he looked like, as this mystery man preferred to remain in the background. Bette, however, was well aware of Stein's keen business acumen and deal-making genius.

When her meeting with Stein was granted, she pleaded with him to join her and the others in creating a successful, well-functioning Canteen. At first he was reluctant, as participation could mean that, for the first time since forming MCA in 1924, he could be cast in the limelight. Bette assured him that it would not be necessary for him to make any public appearances. She needed him as an organizer and financial advisor, not as a front man. Bette could be enormously persuasive when she argued, and Jules Stein finally agreed to become the Canteen's business manager. Years later, Davis said, "Without Jules Stein, there would never have been a Hollywood Canteen."[1]

With Stein on board, the Canteen's newly-elected officers and directors set up an agenda of what needed to be done — from acquiring a building to establishing the basic structure of an organization. Bette Davis and John Garfield agreed to find the right property to house their new Canteen.

Everyone felt that the Canteen should be operated by and staffed with volunteers solely from the entertainment industry. Anyone affiliated with the studios and related guilds and unions would be welcomed — and fingerprinted and photographed, as required by the F.B.I.

The Canteen was to be used exclusively by enlisted servicemen of the United States and Allied Nations. No military officers would be permitted on the floor at any time; civilians who were not connected with the entertainment business would also be prohibited.

The Canteen's officers and directors believed that a serviceman's uniform was his ticket to admission. Everything at the Canteen should be free to him, including food, beverages (no alcohol allowed), and cigarettes. There would never be a charge for entertainment, either — such as the music of top name bands and singers — nor for celebrity autographs, or dancing with movie stars and hostesses. To provide all the free food, drink, and cigarettes, donations were to be sought from Southern California food distributors, which would be the responsibility of whoever became chairman of the Food Committee.

Because the Canteen would be run by people with nine-to-five jobs, its hours would be from 7:00 pm till midnight, in two shifts, Monday through Saturday, and on Sunday, from 2:00 in the afternoon to 8:00 pm.

It was figured that approximately three hundred volunteers would be needed nightly. These would include junior and senior hostesses, busboys, kitchen help, doormen, cloakroom clerks, stage staff, band members, and celebrities who would hand out sandwiches and coffee, as well as provide entertainment.

Poster for The Talk Of The Town, *the film which premiered to raise money for the Canteen.*

The first two nightly shifts would work from 7:00 pm to 9:30 pm; the second from 9:30 to midnight. There would be two Officers of the Day, one for each shift, to greet the servicemen and see that the evening's activities ran smoothly.

Numerous committees were established — some comprised of several members; others having only one or two — each headed by a Chairman. One of the first to be formed was the Building Committee, under the guidance of Al Ybarra, associate art director for producer David O. Selznick. It would face the Herculean task of remodeling the building that Bette and John were to find. Other committees included those for Hosts and Hostesses, Entertainment, Music, Food, Publicity, and Maintenance.

Sometime in July of 1942, Bob Taplinger approached Bette Davis and John Garfield about having a fundraiser for the Canteen. Taplinger, who was the head of publicity for Columbia Studios, suggested selling a "double ticket." The holder would have a seat at the premiere of Columbia Pictures' hot new movie, *The Talk of the Town* (1942), staring Cary Grant, Jean Arthur and Ronald Colman, then go on to the world-famous Ciro's nightclub on the Sunset Strip for an evening of dining and dancing. Each ticket would sell for five dollars, and all proceeds from the event, including the purchase of drinks for a dollar each at Ciro's, would go to the Hollywood Canteen.

Generosity toward the cause was overwhelming. Columbia donated the premiere, Fox-West Coast Theaters turned over the use of its Four Star Theater, and Billy Wilkerson, who owned the popular trade paper, *The Hollywood Reporter*, as well as Ciro's, offered his restaurant.

Everything about the big night of August 28th was unique. Unlike typical Hollywood premieres, this one had no blazing searchlights in front of the theater, circling their beams across the skies. It was wartime, and the huge lamps had been commandeered for military use in detecting possible enemy air attacks. (As a precaution against such attacks, public and commercial lighting in general had been "dimmed out" too.)

Even though bright arcs couldn't announce the glamorous gala over the city, the atmosphere was no less crackling with excitement. "Everyone, including the most sophisticated premiere patron, was aware that something was happening in Hollywood that had never happened before."[2]

The fundraiser was indeed a benefit — not only *for* the Canteen, but *to* many of the people who were part of the event. We have to remember that in 1940s America, racial prejudice was so widespread, it was accepted as a normal part of life. There was a slightly different attitude within the entertainment community as discrimination didn't seem to be such an issue while actually working in films or on stage. After-hours socializing between whites and Negroes was another story.

But at the *The Talk of the Town* premiere, "the guests drawn from the fighting forces included 50 Negroes who were seated on equal terms with everyone else"… and among the "stars whose names are household words" were "Negro artists and musicians."[3]

Bette Davis and John Garfield had never gone along with the prevailing concept of inequality between the races. The supper-dance at Ciro's gave Bette a perfect opportunity to take a public stand. When Rex Ingram, a Negro actor who had a supporting role in *The Talk of the Town*, arrived at the Ciro's party, a number of people stood up to leave. There was even a question about whether he would be seated at all, as "No negro had ever crossed the threshold of the noted rendezvous before."[4] But when Bette saw the fracas at the door, she rushed up and insisted on seating Ingram herself. (A few people did leave, but the effect was minimal.) During her welcoming speech, Davis announced that both the party and the Canteen itself were for all races. Another landmark was reached when Stuff Smith and his "hot fiddle," got the partygoers jitterbugging all over the dance floor. For Smith and his band — on the bill with the great Benny Goodman — "broke the 'color line' at Ciro's. His was the first negro band that ever played there."[5]

Since there was no reserved seating at Ciro's that night, social barriers in general were eased, even within the Hollywood hierarchy. "The fact that everyone had to sit down wherever he could find a chair operated to engender a feeling of good fellowship and gaiety and surprised everyone, including the management."[6] With so much grand entertainment and warm camaraderie, the guests didn't leave Ciro's till close to five in the morning.

The fundraiser was a success on every level, as $6,500 was collected, which would go to renting and renovating the building that would soon become the home of the Hollywood Canteen.

Hollywood Canteen co-founder Bette Davis addresses the audience at Columbia Pictures' The Talk Of The Town *premiere party at Ciro's nightclub.*

CHAPTER 3
BUILDING A DREAM

Members of the Motion Picture Painters and Artists, Local #644, painted both the interior and exterior of the Canteen.

After weeks of searching for a usable building, Bette Davis and John Garfield found a dilapidated place that had once been a barn right in the heart of Hollywood. Located at 1451 North Cahuenga Boulevard, just south of Sunset Boulevard, the structure had been a series of ill-fated nightclubs. The last was a cabaret-type theater called The Red Barn, where drinks and dinners were served, followed by floor shows and stock melodramas such as *Murder In the Red Barn* and *The Drunkard*.

The Red Barn closed its doors in late 1937. The building remained vacant for five years, until August 25, 1942 — four days before the Canteen's fundraiser — when Bette and John leased it for one hundred dollars a month for the duration of the war, plus six months. As soon as the ink was dry on the lease, the officers set the Canteen's opening for October third, 1942.

Bette Davis described the building that would become the Canteen's own as "one step below an eyesore." [1] We can almost hear Davis delivering what would become her perennially parodied line from *Beyond the Forest* (1946): "What…a…*dump!*"

On the evening of September 3, 1942, Davis headed a gathering of interested people who met by candlelight in the decrepit wooden club. Amidst broken crockery and lipstick-stained cigarette butts from some long-ago night life, the group, which included John Garfield and Al Ybarra, outlined their plans to convert the property into something suitable for servicemen. Their goal was to have the building completed in one month.

It fell to Ybarra, representing the Screen Set Designers Guild, to draw up plans, make sketches, and supervise the construction so that the project could be done — almost without cost — in thirty days. To start things off, Bette and John persuaded fourteen guilds and unions to donate both labor and materials.

All of Hollywood's motion picture craftsmen unanimously volunteered their services and immediate cooperation. From plumbers, electricians, carpenters, painters, laborers, prop men and teamsters to art directors, decorators and cartoonists, everyone pitched in. In addition, thousands of feet of lumber, multiple barrels of nails, gallons of paint, miles of electrical wire, hundreds of yards of concrete, and scores of plumbing fixtures were freely given.

The old Red Barn was thoroughly ripped apart. Truckloads of new lumber were rolled into place as carpenters tore out and rebuilt floors and walls. Looking like something in a sped-up movie, grips,

Left to right: Jules Stein (standing), Al Ybarra, Bette Davis and John Garfield review Canteen plans in mid-1942.

prop-makers and laborers worked at a breakneck pace to construct a new bandstand/stage, a large service counter, a kitchen facility, a lighting control room, a lobby, and offices.

Everything took shape as planned, and in just a week, the made-over structure was ready for the electricians. New light fixtures, in the form of antique wagon wheels with lanterns, were hung above the Canteen's main room. Thirty-five painters carrying cans of paint showed up on a Sunday, and finished the job in one day.

Some of the most amusing features of the Canteen's new look were the hand-painted murals in the main room. A large one on the north wall, just above the service counter, was a contribution of the Screen Cartoonists Guild. In keeping with the Canteen's western theme, it was called "Cowboy Heaven," and had lively pictures of "things cowboys dream about." Five big mural panels on the opposite wall were done by the Motion Picture Illustrators and depicted such popular legends as "Frankie and Johnny" and "The Shooting of Jesse James." Even the bathroom walls got special treatment and were painted with delicate springtime blossoms by actor/director Richard Whorf.

When the remodeling was done, various studios and many private companies offered whatever furnishings, equipment, and supplies that were needed. Finishing touches — from upholstering seats to hanging stage backing — would continue till just days before the Canteen's opening.

The old Red Barn had been transformed into a welcoming wood-front building, with an entrance sign crafted out of a large hemp rope that spelled out "HOLLYWOOD CANTEEN FOR SERVICEMEN." Inside, the plain, casual Old West décor was inviting — and able to take a beating from heavy service shoes and good-natured crowds ready for fun.

Workers from many entertainment industry guilds and unions volunteered to remodel the former Red Barn Nightclub into the Hollywood Canteen.

Members of the Motion Picture Illustrators Guild painted western-themed murals on the walls of the Canteen's main room.

Preparing for the Canteen's Grand Opening, electricians hang a wagon wheel chandelier from a large beam above the dance floor.

Loretta Young joins volunteer carpenters for a bite of lunch.

Bette Davis visited New York's Stage Door Canteen to pick up some pointers for her Hollywood Canteen venture.

As their mothers look on, Anita Louise, Bonita Granville and Martha O'Driscoll are signed up as hostesses. Sitting at the left typewriter is Doris Stein, who devoted years of service as chairman of the hostesses.

Before the Grand Opening, three servicemen install the famous rope sign above the main entrance on Cahuenga Boulevard. The sailor is Yeoman Seymour Rice.

CHAPTER 4
FRIENDS IN HIGH PLACES

Rita Hayworth leaves the Canteen after spending an afternoon helping with preparations for opening night on October 3, 1942

Three days after the bombing of Pearl Harbor on December 7, 1942, the Screen Actors Guild formed the Hollywood Victory Committee. Its purpose was to provide a way for actors and actresses to contribute to the war effort through bond drives and various venues to boost the morale of the troops. The Committee was in charge of granting the Guild's permission for actors to make personal appearances at camp shows and other sites for entertainment, waiving established union rules regarding usual compensations and procedures.

Soon after she organized the Hollywood Canteen, Bette Davis met with members of the Victory Committee, which included some of Hollywood's most illustrious and powerful stars. She asked for, and received, their consent to be able to call actors and actresses directly, without having to refer each and every request to the Victory Committee first. This agreement was vital for the Canteen to function efficiently, as its committees could then quickly round up stars without the Victory Committee having to act as a middleman.

As the Canteen's opening night was approaching, Bette Davis, John Garfield, and their fellow officers were considering ways to make the most of the event. After several meetings, Jules Stein came up with an ingenious idea that would not only raise money for the Canteen, but draw dramatic attention to it at the same time. They would, he suggested, have a premiere in reverse.

Stein's plan was to erect bleachers on both sides of the Canteen's outside entrance; tickets for seats in these stands would be sold, at $50 each, to movie stars, studio executives, and community leaders. The premiere would be in reverse inasmuch as the celebrities and executives would be the fans sitting in

Marlene Dietrich and French actor Jean Gabin, register as hostess and host on the day of the grand opening.

the bleachers, admiring the servicemen — the true stars — as they walked into the Canteen. If it was a sell-out, the Canteen could put $10,000 into its coffers.

Everyone loved Stein's concept and arrangements were quickly made to build the bleachers. Canteen officials controlled the ticket sales to insure a perfect mix of stars, executives, and civic leaders. A Servicemen's Committee was also formed with representatives from the Army, Navy, Marine Corps and Coast Guard. They helped plan the opening ceremonies and sold tons of tickets all over town — especially at the studios — thanks to the enthusiastic support of the entertainment industry.

In mid-September, a luncheon was held at the Ambassador Hotel to enlist the backing of civic and religious groups. Filling in for an ailing Bette Davis, Irene Dunne told a packed audience about the agenda for the Canteen's opening on October third. Dunne went on to describe some of what would be offered on regular evenings as well: two big-name bands, three floor shows, dances with pretty Hollywood hostesses, sandwiches and beverages, and a continually open snack bar. This was the first time for members of the general public to learn details of the Canteen's proposed daily operations, and the Ambassador guests were delighted.

With assistance from Yeoman Seymour Rice, starlet Leslie Brooks hangs a sign announcing the opening of the Canteen.

CHAPTER 5
"ALL OF HOLLYWOOD IS YOUR HOST"

Hundreds of celebrities, civic leaders, and various dignitaries listen to Ginny Simms sing during the Canteen's Grand Opening ceremony.

Excitement kept rising as each day brought the opening closer — not only among the Canteen's inner circles, but also within Hollywood at large. A vigorous publicity campaign, headed by publicist, Mack Millar, had been whetting appetites; above all, the boys on the military bases were kept in the know about all things "Canteen." Now word was out that several thousand servicemen might show up, along with hordes of civilians hoping to catch glimpses of their favorite movie stars. Of course private citizens could not be admitted inside the Canteen. But what about the unnerving prospect of having more servicemen than there was space? These boys who would have traveled so far to be part of the opening festivities must not be disappointed.

In anticipation of an overflow crowd, arrangements were made to rent Stoke McGraw's Shell Gas Station next door, at the corner of Sunset and Cahuenga. With its large parking area, the place was converted into an open-air dance pavilion. Here servicemen could jitterbug and foxtrot with hostesses to the music of bands which would alternate between the Canteen proper and the "annex." Renting the gas station was a brilliant move, as the crush of servicemen was even greater than imagined.

On Saturday, October 3rd, 1942, hours before the opening ceremonies were to start, streets near the Canteen had been jammed with star-seekers. Later, in the Canteen's forecourt patio, the bleachers began filling up with celebrities and dignitaries, along with certain enlisted men and commissioned officers who were to be escorts for some of the actresses. Because the Canteen was for the exclusive use of enlisted men, the officers were asked to stay on the sidelines once they walked their dates

With hundreds of servicemen waiting to enter the Canteen, dignitaries filled the bleachers during the Grand Opening ceremony.

inside. Hundreds of servicemen were also packing the forecourt…waiting…wondering…hoping. Then, finally, at 9:00 pm, it was "Showtime!"

With Eddie Cantor as Master of Ceremonies, the dedication program buzzed with a friendly informality, yet a respectful tone for the event's significance was unmistakable; a Color Guard of men from all branches of the Armed Forces officially presented flags to Bette Davis. Thunderous cheers followed Davis' brief speech in which she gave full credit to John Garfield for suggesting that Hollywood establish its own Canteen in the first place.

"Tonight we see our dream come true," Davis said to the servicemen. "This campaign represents an all-out partnership and has exceeded our expectations. I hope all you boys will enjoy yourselves and know that all of Hollywood is your host." [1]

A strong military presence to address the crowd was Colonel Harold D. Shannon, USMC, who commanded the Midway forces: " I feel I speak for every leatherneck, gob, and buck private when I say we are thrilled at this expression of friendship from the men and women of Hollywood…these boys here tonight will be going out to our battlefronts, and in tough moments that may come, they will have a memory of the warm friendliness that is being shown by you folks…" [2]

As the lively M.C., Cantor cracked jokes and introduced Bud Abbott and Lou Costello, who got

Abbot and Costello were among scores of celebrities who entertained the guests during the Grand Opening ceremony.

Hollywood Canteen President and co-founder Bette Davis delivers the Grand Opening welcoming speech.

the guests laughing with their "Who's On First?" routine. Ginny Simms sang "He's My Guy," and Rudy Vallee's Coast Guard Band played several numbers honoring various branches of the Armed Services.

When the dedication ceremonies ended, two hundred uniformed men became the evening's official hosts. They swung open the doors, and thousands of their comrades who had been crammed in the courtyard — and lined up for half a block each way on Cahuenga — entered their Canteen for the first time.

The boys and other guests were instantly caught up into the dynamic atmosphere inside. They saw a huge, inviting wooden dance floor, heard music from the bands of Kay Kyser, Duke Ellington and Rudy Vallee (all of which took turns going over to the "annex" to play for the overflow crowds of servicemen). The young men danced non-stop with a stream of smiling hostesses, and could barely believe their eyes when so many of their partners turned out to be gorgeous film stars.

Show business household names, including a number of Hollywood's most popular actors, seemed to have magically come down off the screen to hand the guys a sandwich or a cup of coffee in between signing thousands of autographs.

Just some of the celebrities who served as hosts and hostesses that night included: Eddie "Rochester" Anderson, Jean Arthur, Anne Baxter, Joan Bennett, Jack Benny, Charles Boyer, Gary Cooper, Joan Crawford, Bing Crosby, Bette Davis, Marlene

Irene Dunne, sitting in the grandstand with servicemen and civic dignitaries, watches the Grand Opening ceremony.

Dietrich, Olivia de Havilland, Irene Dunne, Deanna Durbin, Jean Gabin, John Garfield, Judy Garland, Betty Grable, Cary Grant, Susan Hayward, Rita Hayworth, Marsha Hunt, Veronica Lake, Hedy Lamarr, Mervyn LeRoy, Joan Leslie, Fred MacMurray, Pat O'Brien, Edward G. Robinson, Mickey Rooney, Jane Russell, Randolph Scott, Ann Sheridan, Red Skelton, Robert Taylor, Gene Tierney, Spencer Tracy, Lana Turner, Jane Wyman, and Loretta Young.

Entertainers, such as Eleanor Powell (who danced till she nearly collapsed), pulled out all the stops. Dinah Shore and Betty Hutton sang encore after encore, and Eddie Cantor delivered some of his most famous bits. The servicemen practically tore the place down with their boisterous appreciation.

Although the Canteen was scheduled to close at midnight, the last of the guests and servicemen didn't leave for two more hours. A squad of volunteer janitors — with no one more vigorous than Marlene Dietrich — had to fly into action readying things for the reopening at two o'clock Sunday afternoon.

In addition to all the hostesses, musicians, entertainers, celebrities, and other volunteers, there were three to four thousand members of the Armed Forces who shared in the triumphant opening night of their new Hollywood Canteen.

Servicemen are greeted as they enter the lobby, from which they proceed to the main room for food, dancing and entertainment.

Enthusiastic servicemen and hostesses initiate the Canteen's dance floor on opening night.

Irene Dunne dances with one of the hundreds of servicemen who attended the Canteen's opening night.

CHAPTER 6
DAY IN, NIGHT OUT

Actor Laird Cregar carries a tray of sandwiches from the kitchen to waiting servicemen. Hundreds of sandwiches were served every night.

The old saying, "After ecstasy, the laundry!" certainly applied to the Hollywood Canteen as the glamour of opening night gave way to the reality of daily preparations.

Efforts to get everything ready for the nightly onslaughts of over 2500 servicemen had to be as well-coordinated as military maneuvers.

Each month the soldiers consumed an estimated 4000 loaves of bread, 400 pounds of butter, 1500 pounds of coffee, 50,000 half-pints of milk, 30,000 gallons of punch, 1000 pounds of three varieties of cheeses, 2500 pounds of assorted meats, 20,000 oranges, 100,000 pieces of cake, more than 150,000 sandwiches and hot dogs, 800 pounds of potato chips, 300 dozen doughnuts, 300 gallons of ice cream (for Sundays only), thousands of boxes of raisins, plus cases of jellies, relishes, pickles, mustard, ketchup and mayonnaise.

Preparing and serving the food and beverages was left to the Kitchen and Snack Bar crews. Supervised by committee head, Mary Ford, the first shift of volunteers arrived at noon. In addition to such routine work as making thousands of sandwiches and cutting cakes into hundreds of small pieces, they had to finish washing the previous night's dishes. Later in the afternoon, more volunteers showed up to make the coffee and stock the snack bar with candy, raisins, cigarettes (smoking was permitted outside), and similar items. While all of this was going on, others were sweeping the floors, washing tables, and setting the stage for that night's activities. Mary Ford, wife of Academy Award-winning director, John Ford, was at the Canteen every day early in the morning to be sure that her committee would be on top of things. And she was never above scrubbing tables herself.

Given the number of servicemen expected every night, securing a continuing supply of food and drinks was no easy task. It fell to Italian immigrant, Chef Joseph Leopold Milani, who had established himself in Hollywood as a "celebrity chef." It was on his popular radio show, "Chef Milani" (where he gave cooking instructions to housewives), that Bette Davis had appeared as a guest in August, 1942. When she told Milani of her plans for the Canteen and asked him to direct its food program, he heartily agreed, feeling that it was the least he could do to support the war effort.

The many Southern California food distributors that Milani contacted were extremely generous with their donations. But because of rationing, which the Office of Price Administrations (OPA) instituted after the start of the war, certain food products

Mickey Rooney adds his signature to Chef Milani's jacket. The coat was later sent to the White House and auctioned off to raise money for war bonds.

were in short supply. As meat was a rationed item, and Chef Milani knew he had "to have that stuff" to feed the boys, he went to the OPA and begged for their help. When nothing came of his pleading, the energetic chef shot a telegram to President Roosevelt: "…the Hollywood Canteen will not be able to provide the necessary amount of meat for the servicemen unless we are able to secure an allotment exception permit immediately. Will you please help us secure this permit by directing this wire to the proper authorities with your O.K.? God bless you." He signed it simply, "Chef Milani." Almost immediately, the Hollywood Canteen had all the meat it needed.[1]

Over fifty percent of the Canteen's food and supplies was donated by thirty-five benevolent companies in Southern California. The remaining fifty percent was purchased outright or acquired with ration points. According to Bette Davis' commentary in *Mother Goddam*, the Canteen had a $3,000 weekly food bill.[2]

It would not be Hollywood hyperbole to say that angels helped pay that bill. Since civilians not affiliated with the entertainment industry were barred from the Canteen, a lot of people were left wishing that they, too, could witness the heady mixture of celebrities and servicemen. Wasn't there a way to match their wishes to the Canteen's needs in one fell swoop?

And so was born the Angels' Table, at which four people each paid $25 for the privilege to sit and watch the goings on inside the Canteen. Located on a raised dais in the southeast corner in the back of the main room, and covered with a gold-fringed cloth, the table was sold out every night for weeks in advance. Ouida Rathbone, wife of Basil Rathbone — the "American screen's finest villain and most memorable Sherlock Holmes"[3] — was a tireless volunteer who sold more seats for the Angels' Table than anyone else.

The idea was so popular that a second table was added, which allowed another four people to enjoy the evening's activities — and brought in an extra $100 a night. On average, the Angels' Table (s) generated about $6,000 a month, and was one of the best sources of revenue for meeting the Canteen's operating expenses. (The only other accomodation for special guests — but was not income–producing — was a small room on the second floor where officers and their female companions could look

Sitting at an Angels' Table, actress Jane Withers lights a cigarette for a visiting serviceman.

through a window to watch the night's entertainment. Because the Canteen was for the exclusive use of enlisted men, and no officers were permitted on the first floor, the second floor arrangement was a comfortable solution all around.)

Besides having to cover 50 % of the food budget, reliable income was also needed to maintain a full-time staff of nine people — the Canteen's only paid employees. Occupying an office on the first floor, this group of committed workers, headed by the Canteen's Executive Secretary, Jean Lewin, took care of all the office details, from writing checks to various vendors to putting together and printing "Chatter," the Canteen's weekly publication.

Created soon after the Canteen opened, "Chatter" was a single-page, legal sized mimeographed sheet that was handed out to servicemen as they walked through the doors. It covered entertainment highlights, the following week's schedule of bands, and tid-bits of information about Hollywood. On the bottom of the sheet it advised: "Use reverse side for autographs of your favorite stars, or a letter to your favorite girl — and don't forget the home folks."

"Chatter" also included copies of notes from servicemen or their families. The following excerpts appeared on March 6, 1943:

"Dear Miss Davis: You have incorporated in the Canteen the swell spirit of American friendship and democracy that makes all this worth fighting for."

Pvt. Bernard W. Schoor

Jeanette MacDonald with visitors at a snack table.

Waving to the cameraman, hundreds of soldiers stand on the sidewalk waiting to enter the Canteen.

"The colored soldiers give thanks to you and Mr. Ed. G. Robinson for your services."
                                    Sgt. DeForest Cowan

"My husband is in the Navy. Before he got to the west coast his letters were dull and he seemed to be just a little too homesick. I did all I could in my letters to try to help him but it didn't do too much good. After his visit to the Canteen his spirits were lifted. What I wanted to tell you is how much I enjoyed his visit there."
                                    Margie Canon, Birmingham, Alabama

In the issue of April 20, 1944, there was a letter to "Mom" from "Johnny," that appears to be a staff-written composite; nevertheless, it conveys some of the appreciation felt by every serviceman who ever set foot in the Canteen. One part read:

"I was talking with Billy Grady, a talent scout, and he said that MGM with all its dough didn't have enough to buy the entertainment we guys get for nothing for just one week at the Hollywood Canteen."

The Canteen was turning out to be even more successful than its founders had hoped. It was reassuring to see that all the necessary elements could click in and everyone really could work together and make thousands of G.I.s very happy. There would always be challenges, of course, and each day they would be met. Two examples occurred early on: one was particularly vexing; the other became a crisis.

The Hollywood Canteen had no sooner been formed than the powers that ran New York's Stage Door Canteen got their noses out of joint and called the Hollywood people "copycats."[4] After the exchange of several telegrams and phone calls, the New York contingent suggested that the Hollywood Canteen be regarded as a branch of the Stage Door Canteen. A special meeting of the Hollywood Canteen's officers and Board of Directors was called in mid-August, 1942. While the Hollywood people always acknowledged that co-founder, John Garfield, had drawn his initial inspiration from the Stage Door, everyone at the Hollywood meeting agreed that *their* Canteen would be "Hollywood's own."[5] The Hollywood Canteen would not, in any way, be connected to or with the Stage Door Canteen. This decision was conveyed to the Stage Door officials and things seemed to settle down.

But all did not stay quiet on the eastern front. After the Hollywood Canteen opened, other issues arose. One had the Stage Door people complaining that the exciting radio shows being broadcast from Hollywood were overshadowing those from New York. They felt that Hollywood — having unlimited big-name stars in its own back yard so handy to go on the air — was stealing its thunder. Three weeks after the Hollywood Canteen's opening, stage actress Helen Menken was sent to California by the Stage Door Canteen in an attempt to resolve all their concerns. There are no official records or newspaper articles detailing the points discussed or their resolutions. Things must have been settled amicably, as no further references to any problems were found.

There was, however, a matter far more serious than New York rivalries, and its head was rearing right in Hollywood.

Before the Canteen opened, Bette Davis had appeared before the Screen Actors Guild's Hollywood Victory Committee, which arranged personal appearances of its members for such war efforts as bond drives and entertaining the troops. Davis needed to streamline the Canteen's ability to get SAG members as entertainers for the nightly floor shows. And she had been given the go-ahead to be able to call actors and actresses directly instead of having to put each request through the Committee. Then, a few months after the Canteen opened, Bette was summoned to a meeting of the Victory Committee where she was told that the Canteen could no longer call celebrities directly.

Bette explained that what the Committee was asking would make it impossible to continue running the Canteen. They had to be able to call a Spencer Tracy or a Marlene Dietrich at the last minute and ask them to appear that evening. She reminded the members that they had already agreed, before the Canteen opened, to let them make direct calls and suggested they refer to the minutes of that meeting.

Civilian spectators regularly waited outside the volunteers' entrance, at the rear of the Canteen, to get a glimpse of the celebrities.

The Chairman of the Committee, James Cagney, responded by saying, "regrettably, the minutes of that meeting had been lost," so they were no longer bound by whatever commitment they had made. Davis rose and said, "Mister Cagney, ladies and gentlemen, I will give you until tomorrow to give me back your original permission. If not, I will have no choice but to close the Canteen. I will so advise the forty-two guilds and unions who were part of founding the Canteen. I will send a statement to the press if you do not change your minds by tomorrow morning."[6]

As only Bette Davis could, she turned and left the room. Everyone on the Committee knew that the mighty Miss Davis meant business — especially Cagney, who had made two pictures with her. (Imagining Bette's frustration with Cagney at the Committee meeting, it's easy to think of the scene from *Jimmy The Gent*, 1934, where Davis slaps a rude Cagney across the face during an argument in an office, or the one from *The Bride Came C.O.D.*, 1941, when an exasperated Bette pounds on Jimmy's shoulders — or throws a bucket of water at him.)

At six o'clock the next morning, Davis received a call telling her that the Committee, which had met all night, agreed to let the Canteen continue calling stars directly. Bette could breathe again.

Basil Rathbone introduces busboys, waiters and kitchen help to take their nightly bow for all their hard work.

The jitterbug was, by far, the favorite dance at the Canteen.

Columbia stars Leslie Brooks and Janet Blair have fun in the kitchen.

Actresses Marguerite Chapman and Evelyn Keyes give a round of applause to a dancing G.I.

As she did almost every night, co-founder Bette Davis signs another autograph.

The crowd enjoys one of Basil ("Sherlock Holmes") Rathbone's oratories. He and his wife, Ouida, were dedicated volunteers.

CHAPTER 7
RULES OF THE GAME

FBI regulations required strict identification of all volunteers. Here, Irene Dunne is being fingerprinted at the Canteen.

Without a doubt, some of the brightest jewels in the Canteen's crown were its faithful hostesses. Between 150 to 200 of them were needed nightly to keep the Canteen running; it also took an exceptional person to run the hostesses.

That woman was Doris Stein, "the leader of the pack."[1] She was the wife of Jules Stein, the MCA founder who had been so helpful to Bette Davis with the Canteen startup. As the spouse of such a powerful Hollywood figure, Doris herself became an important presence in the company town. Before the opening of the Canteen, it was Doris, as head of the Hostess Committee, who sounded the call for volunteers throughout the industry, which was met with great enthusiasm.

Once the Canteen was on its feet, Doris, assisted by Florence C. Cadrez, had to be certain that there would be enough hostesses on hand every single night. This meant making numerous phone calls on a continuing basis to various studios, guilds and unions to recruit everyone. Doris also had to set a nightly schedule whereby two different gentlemen — one for each shift — would be available as Officers of the Day. These were usually studio executives who agreed to come to the Canteen to greet the servicemen and generally oversee the night's activities.

The hostesses, grouped into junior and senior categories, included actresses, studio secretaries, wardrobe ladies and other female film industry employees. Junior hostesses were typically in their late teens and early twenties, with vivacious, friendly personalities. It was their job to dance and chat with the servicemen, show them where to get their food and drinks, and keep the welcoming, upbeat rhythm of the Canteen perking along.

Just before the Canteen's opening, Loretta Young signs up as a volunteer.

The junior hostesses themselves were split into two groups, each with a captain. Some of the captains included such young film actresses as Bonita Granville, Evelyn Keyes, Marsha Hunt, Fay McKenzie, Martha O'Driscoll, Frances Rafferty, and Anne Shirley.

Senior hostesses were there to greet servicemen, see them to seats, serve them food at the ever-popular snack bar, and help the junior hostesses with any problems that might arise. They would also try to help ease possible awkwardness or shyness between the girls and the servicemen. According to the flow of the night, there would sometimes be crossovers, when senior hostesses and other female celebrities took on the role of the juniors and danced with the guys.

While all of the volunteers were carefully selected, particular attention was paid to choosing the dancing hostesses, as they would have the closest contact with the servicemen. As per FBI requirements, every hostess, in fact, everyone, from movie star volunteers to salaried office employees, had to be fingerprinted, photographed and issued an identification card — a practice that would continue throughout the Canteen years. (The I.D. card was similar to a latter-day California driver's license, as it bore one's name, address, physical description and color photograph, but in addition to a fingerprint, there was a statement of union and/or guild affiliation.) The junior hostesses were also given shoulder bags and a red cloth armband with "HC" written in blue piping. Wearing either item wasn't really mandatory; the purse soon disappeared and eventually the armband was seldom worn at all.

Canteen general rules applied to all volunteers, but hostesses had to follow additional specific guidelines. The young women were strictly prohibited from leaving the Canteen premises with servicemen at any time. Nor were they allowed to give out their telephone numbers. But there was one acceptable way that a contract actress could respond to a serviceman's request to reach her. Actress Jean Porter, who had been a junior hostess while under contract to MGM, remembers carrying pre-printed slips of paper in her pocket that had the studio's address on them. She and MGM pal, Donna Reed, handed the papers to happy soldiers, sailors and Marines who left the Canteen with hope, knowing they could have some kind of future contact with these enchanting creatures — especially getting their autographed pictures. "Donna and I found that many we met on those nights kept in touch by mail from all over the world; some from hospitals

Name tag and arm band belonging to junior hostess, Julienne Fridner.

and even some from after they got back home. That made us really connected." [2]

No hostess was ever to meet a serviceman beyond the Canteen. The rule against leaving the building with a young man in uniform was easy to enforce; the one about meeting him someplace after hours was harder, so the Canteen relied on the honor system, which, for the most part, worked very well.

Once in a while, there was a hostess who felt that a particular serviceman was so special she couldn't resist seeing more of him. One young woman named Meg Nisbet did just that on a winter night in 1942 when she met Woody Cole, " a tall blond air cadet" as Glenn Miller's music filled the room.

Meg, who was working in the Messenger Department of RKO Studios, had already crossed the line when she had a second dance with Woody, as she knew that dancing more than once with the same partner was discouraged by the Canteen.

Later that evening, after the Canteen had closed, Meg "broke Bette Davis' cardinal rule about dating" and "met that fresh young cadet at the corner of Sunset and Vine and changed my life forever." On Easter Sunday in April of 1943, Meg and Woody were married, but had precious little time together before Woody was sent overseas. On January 12, 1944, after performing heroic action, Woody Cole was killed. Later, in a ceremony for war widows at March Field, the former Canteen junior hostess was handed a number of her husband's medals, including the Purple Heart.³

When the Canteen first opened its doors, over 3,000 stars, players, directors, producers, designers, grips, dancers, musicians, singers, writers, technicians, wardrobe attendants, hairstylists, stand-ins, agents, publicists, secretaries, and allied craftsmen of radio and screen had officially registered as volunteers. By the time the Canteen closed in 1945, this number would swell to almost 6,000.

Upon acceptance, and after being fingerprinted and photographed, each volunteer was issued a list of rules:

1) Scrupulous politeness at all times of all men in uniform is demanded. If there is any difficulty with a serviceman, please report this immediately to the Officer of the Day, who will deal with him. You must not attempt to handle this yourself.

2) Stay in your own department. By doing this, you will not tread on anyone's toes. If anyone asks about working in a department, other than your own, refer them to the chairman of the department they wish information about.

3) No hostess is to leave, at any time, under any circumstances, with a serviceman — or to meet him outside the vicinity of the Canteen. We are responsible, not only to ourselves and to the Hollywood Canteen, but also to the name of the entire Motion Picture Industry.

4) If you, personally, do not appear for three consecutive times on the shift specifically assigned to you, you must, unless you get a special suspension or send an alternate to take your place, relinquish your right as a permanent member of the Canteen and return your identification card to your Chairman.

5) All Committee Chairmen and Captains must make sure that the individual rules pertaining to the particular department are understood and enforced. Arrangements must also be made to replace any last minute emergency dropouts.

6) All volunteer workers, hostesses, hosts, entertainers, musicians, name people, etc., must enter through the Cole St. door. There will be a light there at all times.

7) All workers must register in and out. A registry book will be at the Cole St. entrance. This is most important. Report to your Captain or Committee Chairman after registering.

Beulah Bondi's identification card.

8) The Officer of the Day is the only person in the Canteen who has the authority to deal with any questions, emergencies, criticisms. Report all such to him.

9) Do not high-pressure anyone for anything.

10) Try to be on time at all times.

These were the rules established at the Canteen's outset; over the years there would be changes here and there as real life dictated the need for some modifications or additions.

Some things, however, never changed at all. The original hours proposed for the Canteen were maintained throughout its 38 months of operation. It was open every night from 7:00 o'clock till midnight, and on Sundays from two in the afternoon till eight in the evening.

Though the Hollywood Canteen was, as its entrance sign clearly proclaimed, "for Servicemen," women from all branches of the Armed Forces were also welcome. WACS (Women's Army Corps) and WAVES (Women Accepted for Voluntary Emergency Service, Navy) could occasionally be found dancing and talking with men in uniform, but it was always the male contingent who made up the vast majority of guests. In the beginning, Canteen attendance averaged about 1500 soldiers a night, but it wasn't long till it hit 2500.

On weekdays, servicemen began lining up on the sidewalk in front of the Canteen an hour before it opened; on weekends, they started gathering two, sometimes three, hours early. It was not unusual for a soldier or sailor who came later in the evening to wait outside for as many as three hours.

These were kids from Midwestern farms who had never seen an ocean and were suddenly in the Navy; they were boys from the tenements of eastern cities now walking the palm-lined streets of Hollywood. Some of these young men might have hitchhiked from military camps as far as one hundred miles away. Some would be shipped out the next morning for places unknown, and, as the war continued, some would be coming back from such battlefronts as Guadalcanal, Midway, and Iwo Jima.

The official fire regulations limited the Canteen's maximum capacity to 500 people, but that number was always exceeded. In fact, there were probably about six to seven hundred servicemen, plus one hundred and fifty volunteers occupying the building at any one time. To prevent extreme congestion and to accommodate as many soldiers as possible, a system was devised by which the boys would enter and leave in shifts of about five hundred. Inside, the master of ceremonies for the evening's entertainment would tell the crowd, "Fellows, we hate to do this, but a thousand of your buddies are outside [waiting] to see the show. We're going to ask all of you who have been here an hour or so to leave now, so they can come in." [4]

There never seemed to be any grumbling among the men, no matter how hot the band, or how cute the junior hostesses. They would pick up their caps at the checkroom, say thanks to a senior hostess and an Officer of the Day, then head up Cahuenga, comparing autographs or the vocal stylings of Martha Tilton and Ginny Simms. The line of waiting servicemen outside would enter the forecourt, divide into twos, sixes and dozens, until four or five hundred newcomers joined the action inside. They, too, enjoyed all the benefits of the Canteen, till, after about an hour, they headed for the exits so that others could take their places.

Paulette Goddard sits on the dance floor with servicemen and hostesses to watch the nightly floor show.

Making room for dancer Bill "Bojangles" Robinson, the audience is spellbound by his unequaled tap dancing.

Kay Kyser leads his band while a hostess and soldier dance the hula. Kyser's band played almost every Saturday night at the Canteen.

Actress Ann Southern and columnist Louella Parsons are called up on stage during a nightly floor show.

Eddie Cantor, who was Master of Ceremonies at the Canteen's Grand Opening, entertained on a regular basis.

CHAPTER 8
"WHAT STARS WILL BE HERE TONIGHT?"

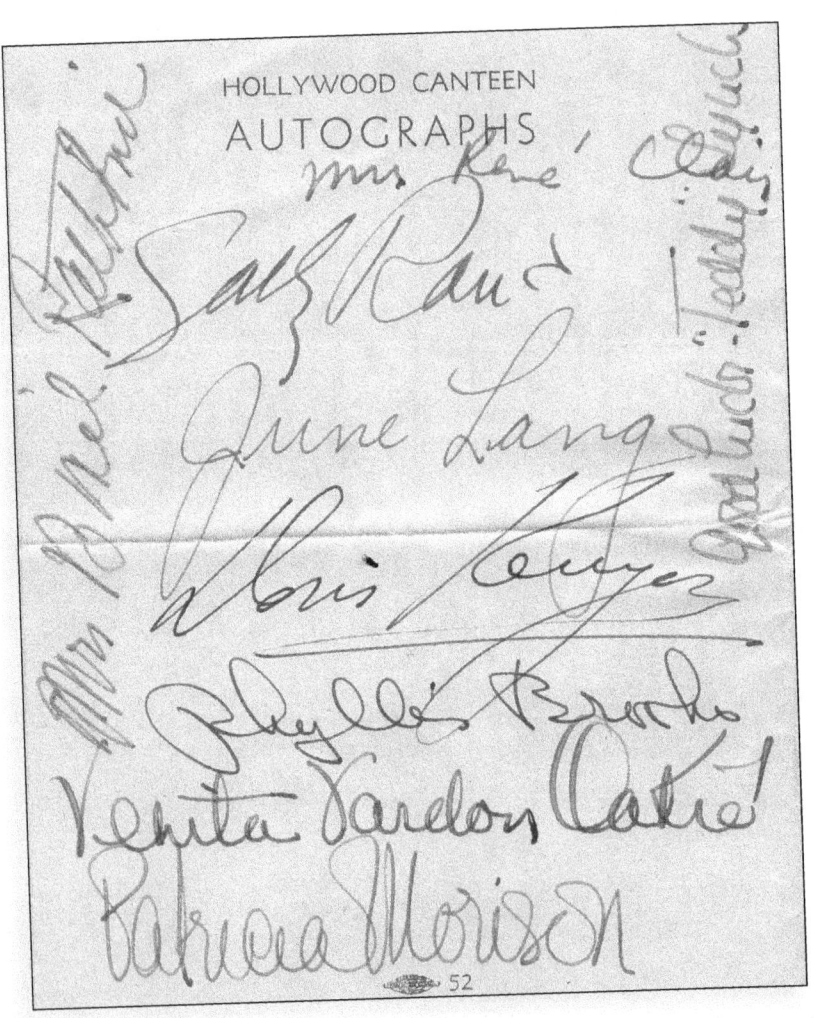

Some celebrity volunteers' autographs.

Once the servicemen walked through the Canteen doors, they hit the snack bar as fast as they could, where they were served by some of Hollywood's most recognizable and generous stars.

Actresses such as Irene Dunne and Linda Darnell not only offered food and coffee, signed endless autographs and posed for countless pictures as boys passed their cameras around, they also repeatedly answered questions about their own lives. Glamour girls were kept on their toes by going back and forth to the kitchen and supply room, replenishing the food, drink and other items as quickly as they were consumed.

While the senior hostesses were running the snack bar, their male counterparts were acting as hosts, busboys, and kitchen staff. Top stars, leading men, grand thespians, character actors, all pitched in. Servicemen reached for sandwiches from enormous trays wielded by Spencer Tracy and Robert Benchley. They returned the smiles of stately Basil Rathbone or elegant Herbert Marshall coming out of the kitchen in their big white aprons, and laughed at comedians Buster Keaton and Red Skelton bussing tables.

Perhaps the greatest gift the male celebrities gave to the servicemen was to sit down with them at one of the tables — and just talk, man to man. Actors such as Paul Henreid and Canteen co-founder John Garfield were especially sought after as they patiently listened to the concerns of the young men.

One night in 1944, the servicemen were delighted with a surprise visit from United States Vice President Henry Wallace, who joined other volunteers helping out in the kitchen. The informal, friendly atmosphere of the Canteen made it easy for the boys to kibbitz with anyone, even someone high in the White House.

Joan Crawford really loved signing autographs for the boys.

Almost always, the first question that a wide-eyed soldier would ask the minute he entered the Canteen was, "What stars will be here tonight?"[1]

Whether the ones he encountered on a particular evening had the biggest names or were some personal favorites who just appealed to him, an excited serviceman was very rarely disappointed. Maybe the singer on stage is the one whose records a guy used to play and play before he joined up — and now that familiar voice is saying, "Hi, soldier" right to *him*. And the junior hostess smiling at the shy sailor is the starlet whose movies he never missed — and the next thing he knows, he's dancing with her.

The most regularly spotted famous face was that of Bette Davis. Not only was the dynamic star of such powerful films as *Jezebel* (1938) and *The Letter* (1940) consistently on the scene, often performing in skits with other entertainers, but as the Canteen's co-founder and responsible president, she was all over the place — keeping things humming, putting out fires. "When one is working with volunteers," she said, "one's hands must never be idle."[2] Jean Porter remembers Davis treating her (and other hostesses) "like a sister," and when she had to "enforce a rule, she did it in a nice way. Oh, she was wonderful!"[3]

Certainly one of the most beautiful faces the enlisted men found at the Canteen was Hedy Lamarr's. "Some nights," Lamarr wrote in her autobiography, *Ecstacy And Me,* "I signed so many autographs I thought my arm would drop off, but I couldn't resist those boys…I remember one night a slim boy with glasses, no more than nineteen, said, 'I leave for overseas next week and now I've

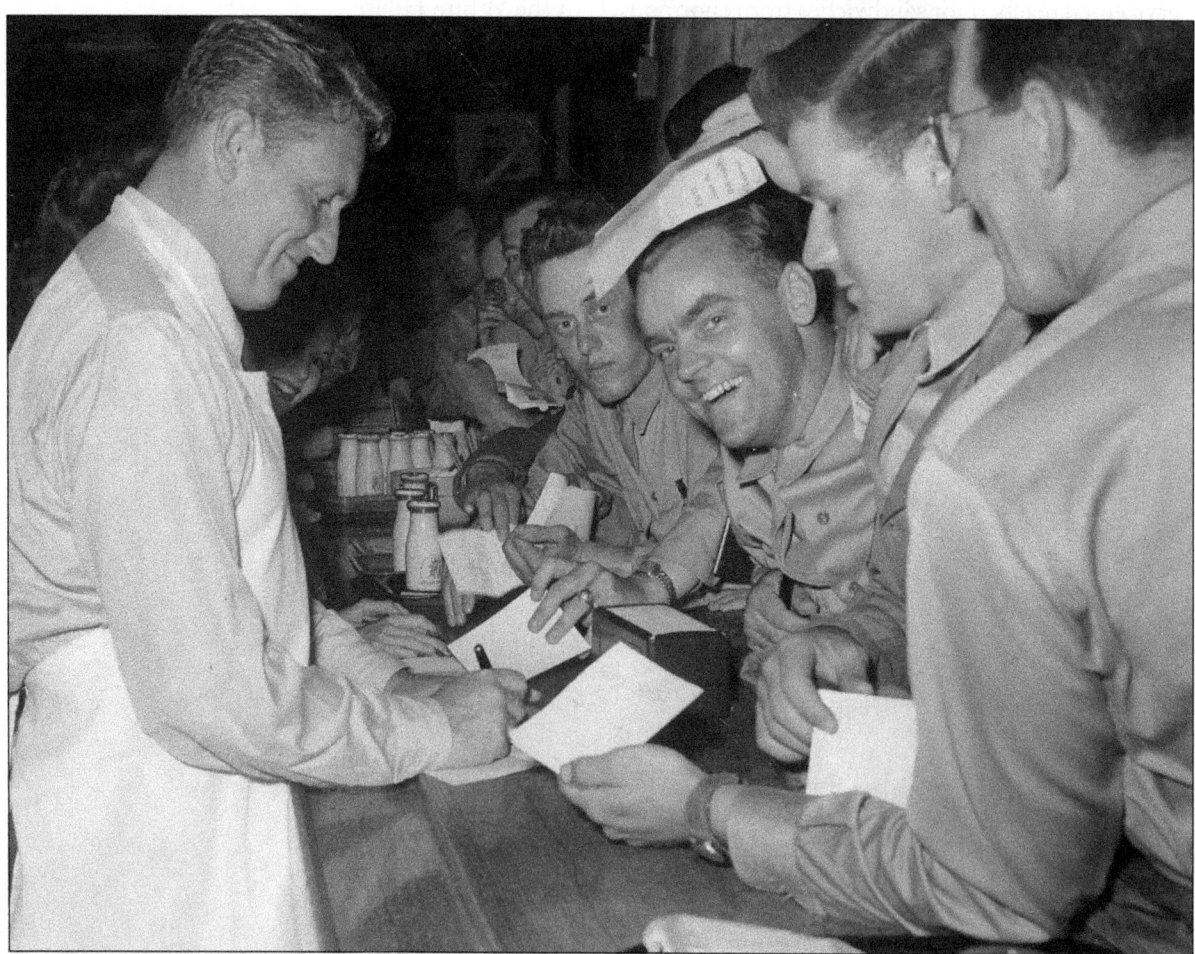

Spencer Tracy was always besieged by autograph-hungry fans.

got something to live for. Wait till I get home and show the neighbors your autograph.'"⁴

"What stars will be here tonight?" Stars that made a family: everybody's mother-grandmother-aunt character actresses Beulah Bondi or Mary Gordon; teenager Roddy McDowall — *Lassie Come Home* Roddy, looking kind of like that younger brother back home.

What stars? Larger than life movie queens? Absolutely. And yet…there was something wonderful — intimate, really — in seeing Marlene Dietrich with barely any makeup on, and discovering that Joan Crawford wasn't as tall as she looked on the screen. And because the actresses dressed casually — even the most sophisticated beauties left their evening gowns in their closets — they seemed somehow so…*accessible*.

While the men in uniform were having the time of their lives, the volunteers — from studio secretaries to name-above-the-title celebrities — had their own satisfactions. Yes, it was delightful to know that you were doing something for the war effort that was so hands-on; so instantly gratifying as you saw a boy's reaction to a dance, a joke, a smile. But some stars' rewards would be less obvious.

Just after the Canteen opened, French actor Jean Gabin told Hollywood columnist Sidney Skolsky, "I love doing this," referring to his new kitchen duties. "I don't have to worry about how I look. I don't have to fight with producers and argue with writers about story. I just stay here in peace and no one bothers me."⁵

For Joan Crawford, the dividends went deeper. Though grateful servicemen, had they even thought

Marlene Dietrich and Rita Hayworth serve coffee with a smile.

about it, wouldn't have cared, Crawford's involvement with the Canteen coincided with a fallow period in her career.

Adopted daughter Christina Crawford, reflecting on her mother's Canteen experience, says, "I know she enjoyed it. But I think part of it was that they took a lot of pictures and there were a lot of people appreciating the stars. And at the time, she wasn't working very much, and so I think it filled a void for her that work didn't."[6]

Crawford had done only three movies during the Canteen years — including *Hollywood Canteen* (1944), in which she appeared with many other Canteen stars playing themselves. Her last film for MGM, *Above Suspicion* (1943), marked the end of her long contract with that big, prestigious studio; she had not yet been embraced by Warner Bros., nor given the movie that would change everything for her, *Mildred Pierce* (1945), for which she would win an Academy Award.

If indeed Crawford's period of down time increased her commitment to and availability for the Canteen, it was a good deal all around. Whatever the motivation, Crawford clearly relished being a hostess, and the boys were thrilled that she was one.

When she got ready to go to the Canteen, she must have conveyed her sense of the place's glamour and importance. For Christina remembers that as her mother got dressed on her appointed evenings, she let the little girl — who caught the excitement — "dress up in her clothes, including the high heels, and she would put makeup on me. It was hilarious!"[7] Crawford even brought the Canteen home with her,

Bing Crosby always packed the house whenever he performed.

Crooner Frank Sinatra and actress Claudette Colbert perform on an NBC radio show from the Canteen in 1943.

Cary Grant chats with Irene Manning while waiting to get up on stage.

for in the summertime, she had garden parties for the servicemen at her house.

Other stars also went the extra mile — literally — such as Kay Francis, who drove to the Lake Norconian Naval Hospital about 50 miles southeast of Los Angeles, and picked up wounded sailors to bring them to the Canteen. [8]

Of course all the stars — human beings after all who just happened to become famous — were elated knowing that they were doing something worthwhile for the troops. But the Canteen also gave them something more. These were people who worked in the rarified atmosphere of movie studios, and socialized almost exclusively with other celebrities. Mingling with young men from every sort of background offered the stars a semblance of normalcy, and a unique sense of community they otherwise could not have had. [9]

Yes, Hollywood entertainers, including Canteen volunteers, did have contact with servicemen when they performed at camp shows or visited hospitals, but only the Canteen provided them such varied interactive socialization.

Volunteering at the Canteen must indeed have been its own reward. Many of the actresses had been awake before dawn and worked long hours in high heels and heavy makeup under hot lights at the studio — yet, at the end of the day, off they'd rush to the Canteen to dance the night away. Then there were the talented entertainers like Jean Porter, who sang for the soldiers from the Canteen's stage on Tuesdays and served them food and danced with them on Thursdays. Now and then she would stay for two shifts; sometimes she showed up on Sundays and for special occasions, too.

After more than sixty years, the still vivacious Porter reminisces about her hectic schedule: driving from MGM days in Culver City to Canteen nights in Hollywood, smiling, singing, dancing, serving. "Don't you realize how much *fun* that is? That's not work. I looked forward to going to the Canteen! The guys were so sweet. They were so grateful. And most of them kept in touch." She treasures all the letters she received from the servicemen and has delighted in sharing them with her granddaughter. Porter, who recalls the Canteen as a place of "total happiness for everyone who was in there," says she can "even still smell it — the wood floor, the good food." [10]

Other long ago volunteers also continue savoring the Canteen phenomenon. Actress Marsha Hunt was "Captain of a team of hostesses, phoning and reminding 20 young women what their shift hours would be, and finding substitutes for any who couldn't be there." [11]

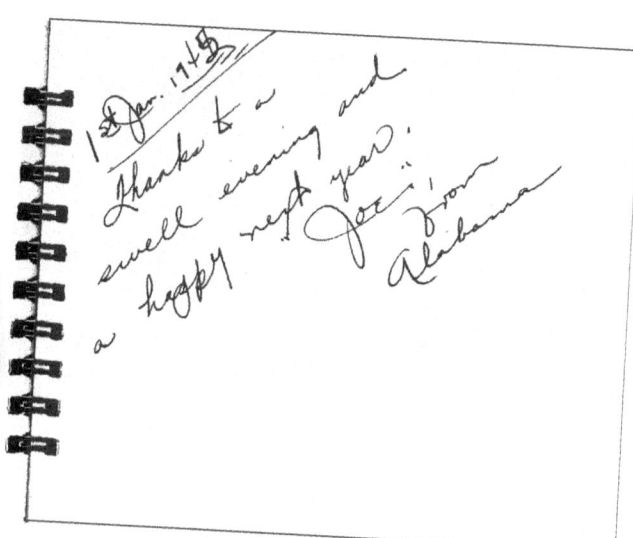

Above: Autograph books were handed out to servicemen and volunteers. Right: A serviceman's entry in a hostess' autograph book.

Playing the drums, multi-talented Mickey Rooney was a crowd-pleaser.

Over sixty years later, remembering the Canteen's servicemen, Hunt says, "Bless their hearts, I've met so many of them since — in all walks of life. I met a number of them on a commemorative cruise on the fiftieth anniversary of Pearl Harbor. I danced with some of the dear old boys — as I was a dear old girl — and so many of them told me that they had danced with me or gotten my autograph at the Hollywood Canteen." [12]

One of Hunt's fondest — and far-reaching — connections from her Canteen years involved a fellow who was not in the Armed Forces at all; he handled the cars of the volunteers who parked behind the Canteen. Gerald Hamilton was "a young Negro — and a personality kid. He remembered my car and always ran and got it when he'd see me coming out the back door to go home." [13]

A few years after the war, Hunt bumped into Gerry who was again parking cars, when he told her that he was heading for New York to study opera. Some time later, "he turned up backstage when I did my first play– and all my other plays — on Broadway. He was by then an opera singer, a concert singer…and we became lifelong friends. He called me 'Princess.' I knew him so well over the years…he helped enrich my life. He even sang a song I had written on one of his concert tours, and that enabled me to join ASCAP as a songwriter! So you see," Hunt says, so many years after she met Gerry, "there are all kinds of highlights connected with the Canteen." [14]

During the war, the average American went to the movies about twice a week and members of the Armed Services, stationed at home or abroad, saw all the latest Hollywood films that were immediately

Linda Darnell (second from left) and Claire James (third from left) were among hundreds of hostesses who served coffee and food at the snack bar.

shipped to them directly from the studios. Hunt, who had made nearly twenty pictures before 1942, and kept filming throughout the Canteen duration, was a popular screen personality. She would have been an asset to the Canteen in any event, but she provided a bonus as well.

Because actors and actresses worked a six-day week, Saturday night was their only chance to go out on the town, attend parties, and stay up late, since they could sleep in on Sundays, their one day off. This made Saturday the hardest night for the Canteen to get celebrities. But Marsha was married to a man "in uniform away from home and I had time on my hands." She recalls that many Saturday nights, "I was the only young face familiar" to the servicemen. "I signed my silly name thousands of times every Saturday night."[15]

Hunt not only gave generously of herself to the Canteen, she recruited her sister Marge as a hostess, her mother for food preparation and her father as a busboy.

Volunteering also became a family affair for other stars when a group of their mothers worked together in the kitchen and at the snack bar. Just some of these included the mothers of Joan Crawford, Lou Costello, Frances Dee, Betty Grable, Bonita Granville, Anita Louise, Jeanette MacDonald, Fred MacMurray, Roddy McDowall, Ann Miller, Pat O'Brien and Claire Trevor. Wives of such actors as William Bendix, Ronald Colman and Basil Rathbone joined in, too, as did the sisters of Joan Leslie and Roddy McDowall. A serviceman could feel that his encounter with Hollywood was all the more remarkable, sitting and chatting with a favorite movie star's *mom*.

What stars will be here tonight? Ones whose handclasps and smiles the boys would remember on battlefields and in hospitals and for the rest of their lives. And stars who would remember the boys for the rest of their lives, too.

Popular singer Kate Smith never disappointed her audience.

Hollywood Canteen co-founder John Garfield chats with servicemen.

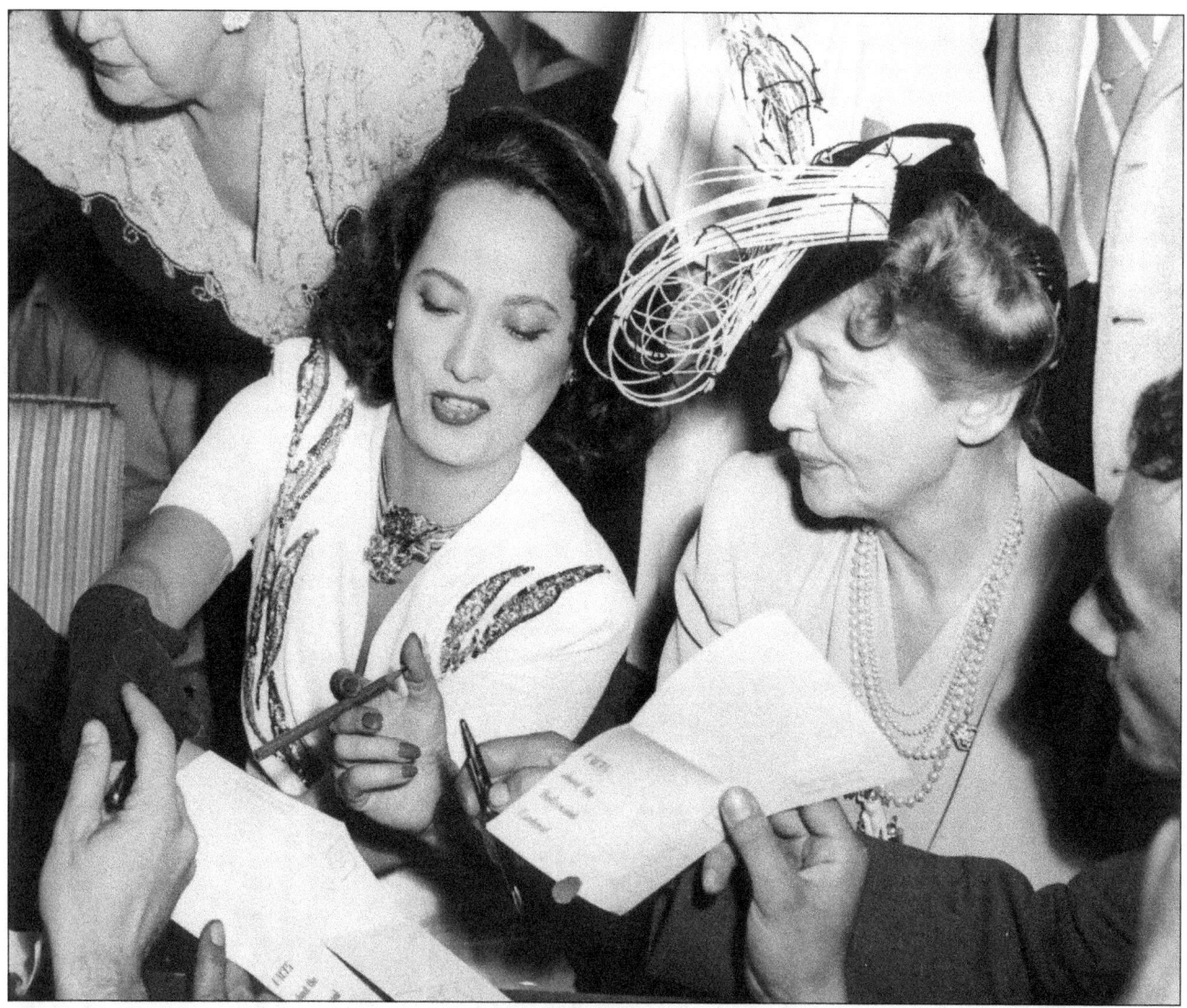
Merle Oberon and Hedda Hopper sign autographs.

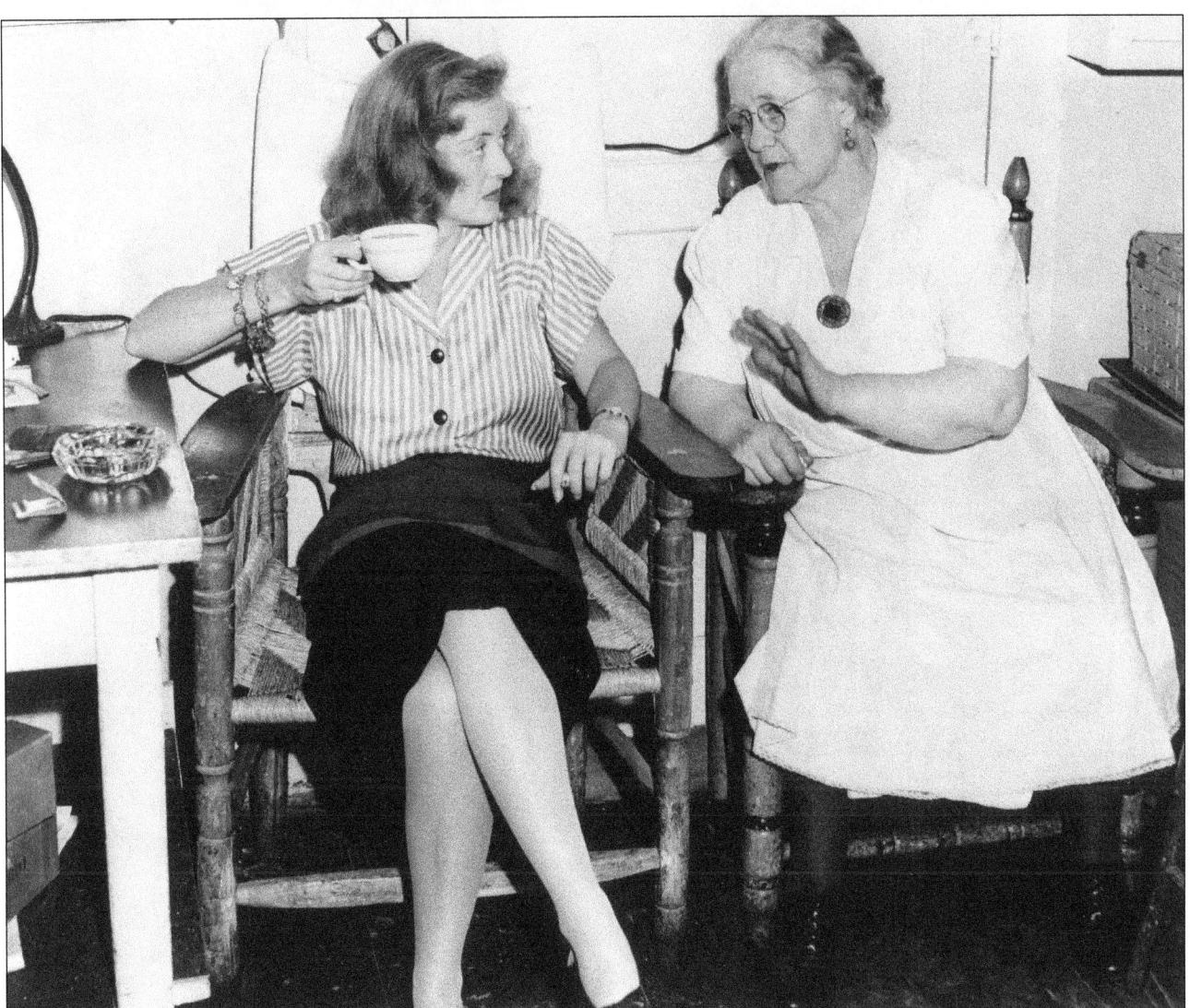
Canteen President Bette Davis and character actress Mary Gordon, take time-out for a cup of coffee during the nightly activities.

Admiring fans enjoy Dinah Shore's rendition of one of her popular songs.

The boys were mesmerized when Spencer Tracy got up on stage and simply talked to them.

Tommy Dorsey and his band played several times in the Canteen's three-year history.

Regular volunteers Marlene Dietrich and Jess Barker pause between nightly floor shows.

Veloz and Yolanda dance for servicemen and hostesses who crowd the edge of the dance floor.

Cary Grant relished bantering with the people in his audience.

Paulette Goddard in a sea of servicemen.

CHAPTER 9
"MISS HAYWORTH, MAY I HAVE THIS DANCE?"

Smiling Rita Hayworth loved entertaining and dancing with the servicemen.

Without the photographs and newsreels, it would be hard to believe that so many servicemen could crowd onto the Canteen's dance floor. But cover the floor they did, as that was where all the pretty hostesses were ready, willing and able to become their partners.

Every night, two bands played their top-of-the line music for hundreds of couples jammed together as they managed to move around. Romantic rhythms such as "Stardust," "You'd be So Nice To Come Home To," and "Moonlight Serenade," were perfect for talking and flirting, but the lively tunes like "Dance With a Dolly," "Boogie Woogie Bugle Boy," or "Chattanooga Choo Choo" were the ones everyone asked for the most so they could do their favorite dance: the Jitterbug. The guys were so crazy about it, as one hostess remarked, "They just jitterbugged you to jelly." [1]

The term, "Jitterbug," had many variations, such as the Lindy Hop, Shag, New Yorker, Collegiate, Hurricane, Boogie Woogie, Suzy Q, and Bombing — and all were exploding at the Canteen.

One night, on a cleared dance floor, Jane Withers put on a Jitterbug exhibition with five eager young men — who were all totally exhausted by the time they had finished. Later, when bandleader Kay Kyser called on Jane to repeat the entire routine up on the stage, she hopped right to it with the same crackling Withers gusto. [2]

Hostess and professional dancer Diane Meredith recalls that everyone would step back and make a circle around the really great jitterbuggers to applaud and cheer them on. "Sometimes I was one of them," she says. " I was not that agile to be flown into the air, but I did a lot of the movements pretty well because we'd been trained to do them." [3]

There was, however, one sour note to the Jitterbug saga. In 1943, a junior hostess named Florida Edwards filed a lawsuit against the Canteen, alleging that she was injured while jitterbugging on October 31st, 1942. Asking for $17,500, Miss Edwards claimed that a young Marine started dancing the Jitterbug with her without her consent. She claimed that he threw her into a spin and when he failed to catch her, she fell on the base of her spine, dislocating her coccyx and wrenching her vertebrae.

Miss Edwards, who considered herself an "Icky" (someone who doesn't jitterbug), denounced the dance. "Jitterbugging is a very particular dance. I don't like it. It reminds me of the jungle antics of natives. They whirl you, pick you up, raise you up in

6 foot tall actress Bunny Waters towers over soldier 5'3" Henry Pilla during a slow dance.

the air, or they spread their legs and take you by the waist and slide you under their legs." [4] During the two-day trial, both sides had "jive experts" testify to the danger or harmlessness of the Jitterbug.

After considering all the evidence, Superior Judge Henry M. Willis ruled against the Canteen and awarded Miss Edwards $8,170. Elaborating on his decision, Judge Willis stated, "The Canteen did not furnish Miss Edwards with safe employment and permitted a jitterbugging enthusiast to indulge in his crazy ideas of dancing with the plaintiff as a helpless victim."[5] Upon hearing the Judge's decision, Miss Edwards exclaimed, "I'm not a floogie-boo (worry-bird) anymore."[6] The Canteen appealed, and when the case was finally heard by the State Supreme Court in 1946, the lower court's decision was upheld. However, Miss Edwards' award was reduced to $7,000.[7]

A highly popular feature at the Canteen was the "Tag Dance," which allowed a young man to cut in on a fellow serviceman and start dancing with his partner. To regulate these exchanges, there was an electric sign on the wall to the left of the stage that read, "TAG DANCE." Whenever the sign was turned on — which was about four or five times a night — the place went wild.

It was not unusual for one hostess to have several partners during a "Tag Dance" song. Stars such as Olivia de Havilland or Merle Oberon might be run ragged as they adapted to so many men's individual dance styles in rapid succession while returning every smile. But seeing the delight in each boy's face kept them going — and helped them forget how much their feet ached.

Within the vast sea of junior hostesses, the majority of the volunteers were not famous. Most of the young women who danced or sat and talked with the servicemen were simply "in the business" — from hard workers in unglamorous jobs at the studios and guilds, to extras, dancers, and aspiring actresses hoping for a break.

Still, the dedication (and yes, sacrifice) of well-known, big name movie stars giving their limited time and considerable allure to the Hollywood Canteen was essential for its image, purpose and success. Dramatic actresses who might not have fit

Dancing was a highlight for visiting servicemen each night.

in to a camp show, with its singing, dancing format, felt valued at the Canteen where her simple social dancing meant the world to a lonely sailor.

Some musical stars who served as hostesses also doubled as Canteen entertainers, while others, even though they could sing and dance, chose only to be good partners for the boys.

"I just wanted to dance with the servicemen," remembers Joan Leslie, a particularly committed junior hostess, who volunteered regularly on Tuesdays, and often on other nights as well. [8]

Joan had been singing and dancing on the stage at nine, and appeared in a number of movies as a child and young teenager (under the name of Joan Brodel). She was signed by Warner Bros. in 1941, and when she was only 17, shined opposite Gary Cooper in *Sergeant York* (1942) and James Cagney in *Yankee Doodle Dandy* (1942), two of the most beloved films of the era. Joan would become "Warner Brothers' most written to personality throughout the war...and...the girl thousands of G.I.s wanted to come home to. At the Canteen, they often got their wish." [9] The eight additional pictures she made during the war did not stop her from showing up at the Canteen, where she was driven and picked up by her father.

Joan often went to the Canteen directly from the studio so that she wouldn't be late for her shift. She recalls one night when she had just arrived from the set of *Rhapsody in Blue* (1945), still wearing her "upswing" hairdo. "While I was dancing with one of the servicemen, my hairpins began falling out, and onto the floor, where servicemen started picking them up. I was horribly embarrassed, as my hair

Surrounded by admiring servicemen, Hedy Lamarr signs her name in wet cement in front of the Canteen.

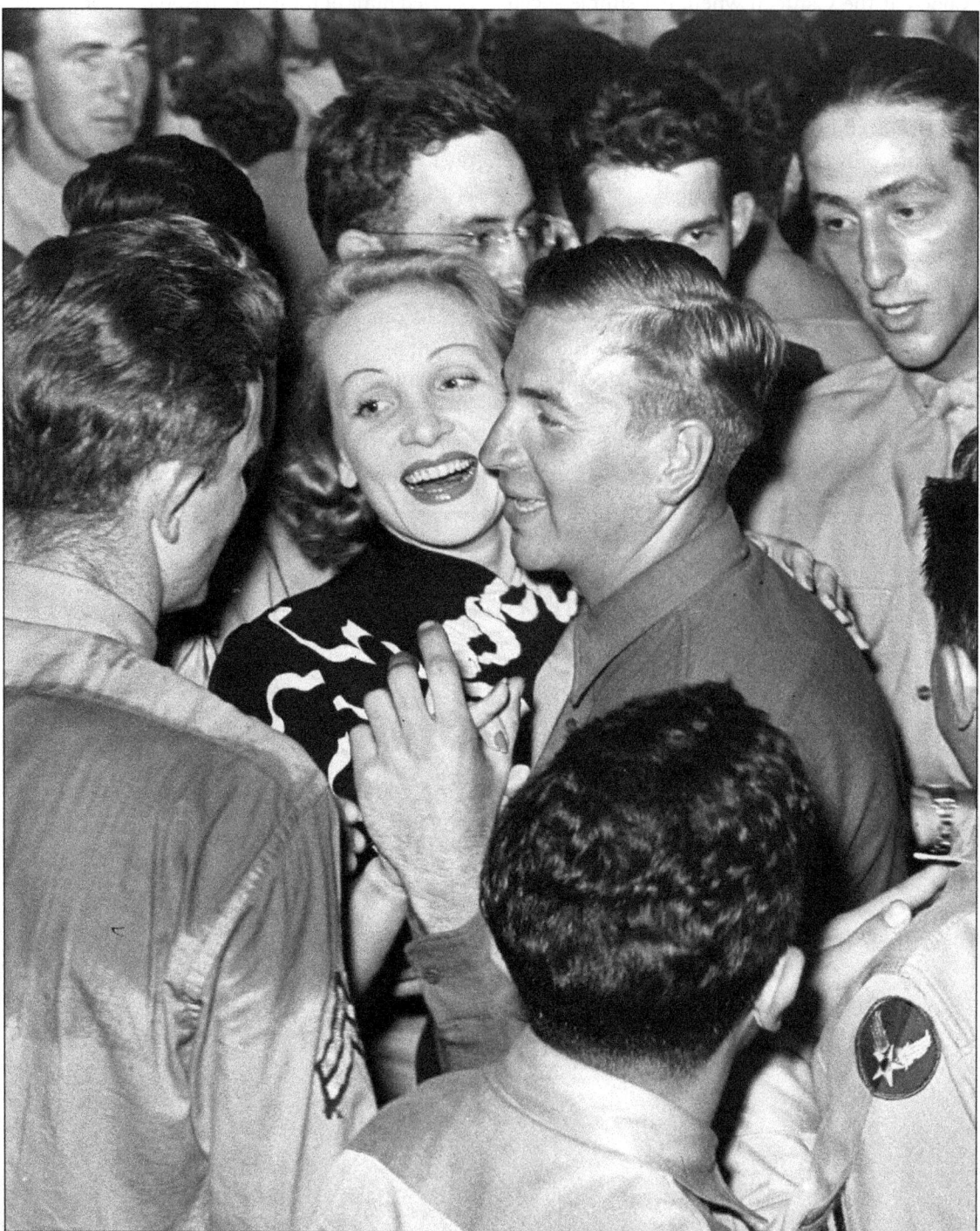
Marlene Dietrich was one the Canteen's most enthusiastic and faithful volunteers.

was coming down on both sides of my head." For a consummate professional like Joan, her reaction is understandable. Not only would the soldiers see a Hollywood star looking disheveled, they could slip on her hairpins that had shot over the floor. Once the boys handed the scooped up pins to the flustered Miss Leslie, she fled to the ladies' room to repair her "do."[10]

Beautiful Joan, with her open, honest, engaging personality, became one of the most sought-after partners of all the dance hostesses. "'Every night I would hear a friendly, 'Hey, Joannie,' from so many corners of the old building. We talked about such simple things, like food, family, and styles. It was so very natural.'"[11] The qualities that made her so popular with the servicemen, combined with her proven acting talent, would make Joan Leslie the perfect choice for the lead in the Warner Bros. movie, *Hollywood Canteen* (1944).

One of the many advantages of a star-staffed Canteen was the variety it offered. If a soldier didn't get to dance with a young, wholesome Joan Leslie, he might find himself pleased to be two-stepping with an elegant Greer Garson — the reassuring "Mrs. Miniver" herself.

A serviceman's heart would be in his mouth when the girl in his arms was Hedy Lamarr. Dancing on air, he could take the very nearness of so much beauty as proof that even in a crazy, war-torn world, marvelous things can happen to him.

Yet the exquisite Lamarr almost didn't step foot on the dance floor at all. As she wrote in her

Dancer Fay McKenzie was a regular at the Canteen — whether jitterbugging with the servicemen or entertaining up on stage.

autobiography, when Bette Davis first asked her to volunteer, she wondered what she could do. Bette assured her, "'Just by being there, you, Hedy Lamarr, will give a big boost to the boys' morale'." But Davis also added that she could help out in the kitchen, sign autographs, and dance with the servicemen.

"I went alone the first night," Lamarr wrote. "This was my adopted land and it had been good to me. But on the way over I told myself I would not dance with the boys. That I would not do. I could never dance with a man unless I cared something for him." However, once Lamarr got involved with the Canteen — where she signed countless autographs and washed mountains of dishes "at least twice a week," she found "I couldn't resist those boys, and, in the end, I was able to dance with pleasure." [12]

Marlene Dietrich was almost a soldier herself. She courageously went into harm's way, entertaining American troops under battle conditions in Europe, for which she would receive the Medal of Freedom. If she wasn't singing or playing her musical saw on makeshift stages, she was practically in the trenches, just to remain close to "her boys."

When she was working in Hollywood, you couldn't keep her away from the Canteen. According to her daughter, Maria Riva, Dietrich and Hedy Lamarr would drive Bette Davis crazy if they spent too much time in the kitchen. "'What is it with you hausfrau?...I need glamour out here!'" [13]

But no one understood better than the sensuous star of such lyrically exotic films as *Morocco* (1930) and *Shanghai Express* (1932), the impact of her visibility. In addition to the scrubbing and cooking, Dietrich certainly was out front, singing from the Canteen's stage, signing autographs and treating the enlisted men to dance after dance. Like all the hostesses, she kept things upbeat for the guys; still "she knew their last dance with 'Marlene' would remain with them through the terrors of war…" [14]

At one point, some of those dances had a unique golden touch. When she was filming *Kismet* (1944), and had painted her legs gold — with real gold paint, not makeup — for a special dance scene, she would arrive at the Canteen to dazzle the young men with those famous Dietrich legs still glittering. Teenage actor (and Canteen busboy) Roddy McDowall remembered Dietrich as being "nuclear, before there was a Bomb. She leveled the place and popped the eyes of every serviceman there." [15]

Though showing favoritism was discouraged by the Canteen, occasionally a bit of string may have been pulled, particularly for a serviceman who was from the Hollywood community, as he was often among old friends. When sailor Harry Carey, Jr. went to the Canteen, it was because he wanted to dance with a certain hostess — the beautiful blonde actress, Gloria Stuart. [16]

Harry, known as Dobe, had a special connection at the Canteen in Mary Ford, wife of director John Ford, and head of the Kitchen and Snack Bar Committee. The Fords had known Dobe since he was born, as his father, the brilliant character actor, Harry Carey, Senior, had worked closely with John Ford on many of his early films. (After the war, Dobe, too, enjoyed a long acting career, which included being a member of Ford's stock company.)

Gloria Stuart — who, more than fifty years later, would receive an Academy Award nomination for her role as the 101 year-old Rose in *Titanic* (1997) — was introduced to Dobe by Mary Ford. Though he had been around Hollywood's lovely ladies all his life, his heart was set on a dance with Gloria and Dobe had his dream come true. But so did countless young men from all over the country, each in his own dream-come-true way, as he went swinging and swaying to exhilarating music, laughing and linked with other charming hostesses.

Then there were the two actresses who ruled as the definitive pin-up girls of World War II — Betty Grable and Rita Hayworth.

We all know their iconic photos, no matter our ages, as they have become emblematic of the war period down through the years. These are the pictures that servicemen pasted on barracks' walls and carried with them into combat. Betty in a white bathing suit, back to camera, smiling at us over her shoulder, standing on those million dollar legs. Rita, posing in bed wearing a black lace and white satin negligee as she looked out from the cover of *Life* magazine (which dubbed her "The Love Goddess").

A soldier attempts to break in on a sailor dancing with actress Claire Trevor during a popular "Tag Dance."

Howard Johnson remembers when, as a young sailor, he saw both Betty and Rita at the Canteen on the very same evening — the ultimate pinup girls right there *in the flesh*. He and a buddy had hitchhiked up to Hollywood from San Diego — "During that war, everybody wanted to stop and take you" — and "was really impressed with the place. The girls there were absolutely gorgeous, and there was a lot of them."[17]

The great Harry James Orchestra was playing, and Johnson got to meet James and his wife, Betty Grable, soon after he arrived. "You wouldn't have known she had a nickel," he says, recalling the phenomenally popular Grable's unpretentious manner. She was warm and friendly, but pregnant, and couldn't dance. So Johnson had a wonderful time dancing with different hostesses, and then, incredibly, the world's most famous redhead was standing in front of him. The next thing he knew, he was dancing with Rita Hayworth, the luscious star of *Blood and Sand* (1941) and *You Were Never Lovlier* (1942), and who would go on to create one of the screen's most radiantly sexy personas in *Gilda* (1946).

Johnson doesn't remember exactly what he said — could it really have been, "Miss Hayworth, may I have this dance?" Nor can he recall any of her words while she chatted with him as they danced; but, he says, she "acted as though she was enjoying it." She struck him as just "glad to be there to help out."

Of course, every other serviceman was trying to cut in. "You'd get beat to a pulp if you tried to go around [the floor] another time. They kept tapping me on the shoulder, wanting me to let her go. And I made up my mind [that] I wasn't going to let her go till I got clear around the floor. And I did!"

Johnson was never able to return to the Canteen, as shortly after his magical night, he shipped out to the South Pacific, where he remained for the rest of the war. When he saw pictures of Hayworth tacked above bunks on his tanker, he'd reflect on his having actually danced with that Ravishing Redhead and become incredulous all over again. "There were probably millions of guys who would have given their eyeteeth to be able to dance with her," Johnson says, "and I felt kind of special that I got the chance to."

As film historian John Kobal wrote of her, "Rita seemed so much to personify all the good things of life worth fighting for…She was an American classic; a heady mixture that enthralled the world."[18]

For five minutes, Howard Johnson held that American classic in his arms. "That particular evening was one of the best things that happened to me all during the years that I was in the service," he says. "It's something you don't forget…In my senior years, it's something to think about."[19]

Whether it was a Foxtrot with a world famous pinup, or a Jitterbug with a girl from the typing pool at Paramount, to a grateful serviceman, a dance at the Hollywood Canteen was always one that ended too soon.

A visiting serviceman becomes "weak-kneed" after Linda Darnell asks him to dance.

A French sailor has a memorable dance with Marlene Dietrich.

Actress and singer Deanna Durbin, dancing with an Air Cadet, was a regular volunteer.

CHAPTER 10
A GOOD TIME FOR ALL: AN INTEGRATED CANTEEN

Following Armed Services policy, servicemen elect to segregate while standing outside the Canteen. However, once inside, all discrimination disappeared.

The Warner Bros. film, *In This Our Life* (1942), presents Bette Davis as a spoiled, willful young woman who kills a child by her reckless driving. She lies to put the blame on Parry Clay, the son of her family's maid, who is immediately jailed. We see Parry's utter despair of anyone believing that he is innocent, as he is a black man in a white world. Parry's reaction on screen reflected racial situations still rampant in 1940s America.

Though discrimination was most obvious in the South, de facto segregation existed throughout the United States. It was just accepted within the dominant society that Negroes (or "coloreds") would be separated from whites — to greater or lesser degrees depending on geography — when it came to schools, restaurants, night clubs, public transportation and housing. And so it was with the Armed Forces.

As they had been in the First World War, Negro soldiers were not only still segregated in WW II, they were relegated to service units supervised by white officers, often working as cooks, cargo handlers, and in other labor-intensive, often hazardous, positions. Though in 1941, at the urging of the National Association for the Advancement of Colored People (NAACP), the War Department slowly began forming all-Negro combat units — including the highly decorated 99th Pursuit Squadron of the United States Army, and the 92nd Infantry Division — black servicemen continued to be placed in low or dangerous jobs.

It would not be until 1948 that President Harry S. Truman would sign Executive Order 9981, which officially desegregated the Armed Forces. However, it was not until 1951 that all branches of the military were integrated.

Bette Davis and Eddie "Santa Claus" Cantor give Cpl. Ernest Anderson the Canteen's mascot during a Christmas Eve stage show.

But during the Second World War, Negroes were fighting double battles as they faced the enemy overseas and prejudice at home. Even in Hollywood, where black actors had been making movies with whites since the early days of motion pictures, segregation prevailed; when the cameras stopped turning, black and white actors did not socialize, nor did the studios employ blacks in offices or on crews.

Given this climate, the Canteen's atmosphere was all the more remarkable. "Significantly," writes California historian Kevin Starr, "the Hollywood Canteen was not segregated, although black and white servicemen tended to remain in their own groups and space."[1]

As she had stood her ground at the *The Talk of the Town* fundraiser premiere, Bette Davis insisted that all servicemen visiting the Canteen be welcomed equally. "As president, I refused to have black GIs put in one section of the Canteen," Davis wrote in *This 'n' That*. "They were free to mingle with the rest. Why not? The blacks got the same bullets as the whites did and therefore should have the same treatment."[2]

Davis and co-founder John Garfield were a united front in their insistence that *all* servicemen would have a good time. For the Negro men in uniform, the reception they received at the Canteen meant even more than a good time. They knew that if it weren't for the Canteen, they could never have enjoyed the easy fraternizing with each other and their white counterparts under one Hollywood roof. And for entertainment, they would have had to travel down to the south central part of Los

In addition to hosting U.S. servicemen, the Canteen also welcomed these French sailors.

Angeles, where they would have been restricted to the night clubs and restaurants that served the black population.

Yet the Canteen was mindful of social relationships between Negroes and whites that had long been held through custom and habit, and so provided both Negro and white hostesses. For the most part, blacks preferred dancing with blacks and whites with whites. But, as Davis acknowledged, the Canteen was aware that potential problems could arise — particularly since many servicemen would have come from the South — and prepared a solution to nip any trouble in the bud. "If an incident occurred," she wrote, "the band was instructed to play 'The Star-Spangled Banner.' We had to resort to that only twice in all the years we operated the Canteen."[3]

Among the many "freebees" that were given out, were thousands of match books with the Canteen's name and logo.

Mickey Rooney, who performed regularly at the Canteen, regales his audience.

An article in the *Los Angeles Times* reported that hostesses were told they were not expected to dance with anyone against their wishes. "Their only instructions were that they show courtesy in refusing an invitation to dance and to be particularly courteous in refusing invitations extended by soldiers of races other than [their] own. It seems that of their own free will some white girl hostesses decided there was no reason why they should not dance with Negro soldiers and some white soldiers saw no reason why they should not dance with Negro girls. They did." [4]

Diane Meredith, a white hostess and MGM dancer, recalls her turn around the floor with a black soldier. As a professional, she liked being partnered with a good dancer –"I thought this guy was great," she says, "and he was." [5]

James Washburn was seventeen when he and some fellow Marines drove up to the Canteen from their base in El Toro. As a child, the young white man had lived with his grandparents in Georgia, where he had been nurtured and loved by the Negroes he knew there. Thinking back on the Canteen, Jim remembers all the great music he heard and all the beautiful hostesses he saw and how happy he was to be in a safe place where he could dance with "the lovely black girls." [6] (According to author Joseph McBride, the Negro hostesses were "recruited by the wife of actor Clarence Muse.") [7]

The *Times* article also pointed out that there had been a faction among some "women acting as 'chaperones' of the hostesses"..."who tried..."to pass a rule forbidding 'mixed dancing'...It is understood that one reason the rule was not passed is because Bette Davis and John Garfield threatened to resign from the board and withdraw the support of the Screen Actors Guild if any such action were taken." [8]

One night, Bette Davis introduced Corporal Ernest Anderson to the audience. He was the black actor whose career Davis launched when he played Parry Clay in *In This Our Life*. Referring to the Canteen's policy of equality, Corporal Anderson said, "I'm grateful for everything. I probably realize this more than you, but I know this is a real democracy and worth fighting for." [9]

When Louis "Satchmo" Armstrong and his wonderful band played, it was "standing room only."

Many Hollywood nightclubs sent dancers to entertain at the Canteen.

A GOOD TIME FOR ALL: AN INTEGRATED CANTEEN

As Duke Ellington is on stage with Kay Kyser, Jack LaRue (with apron) poses with Negro hostesses and servicemen. Racial segregation was never tolerated at the Canteen.

Tireless Marlene Dietrich not only sang, danced, and served beverages, she was fierce about cleaning up.

A GOOD TIME FOR ALL: AN INTEGRATED CANTEEN

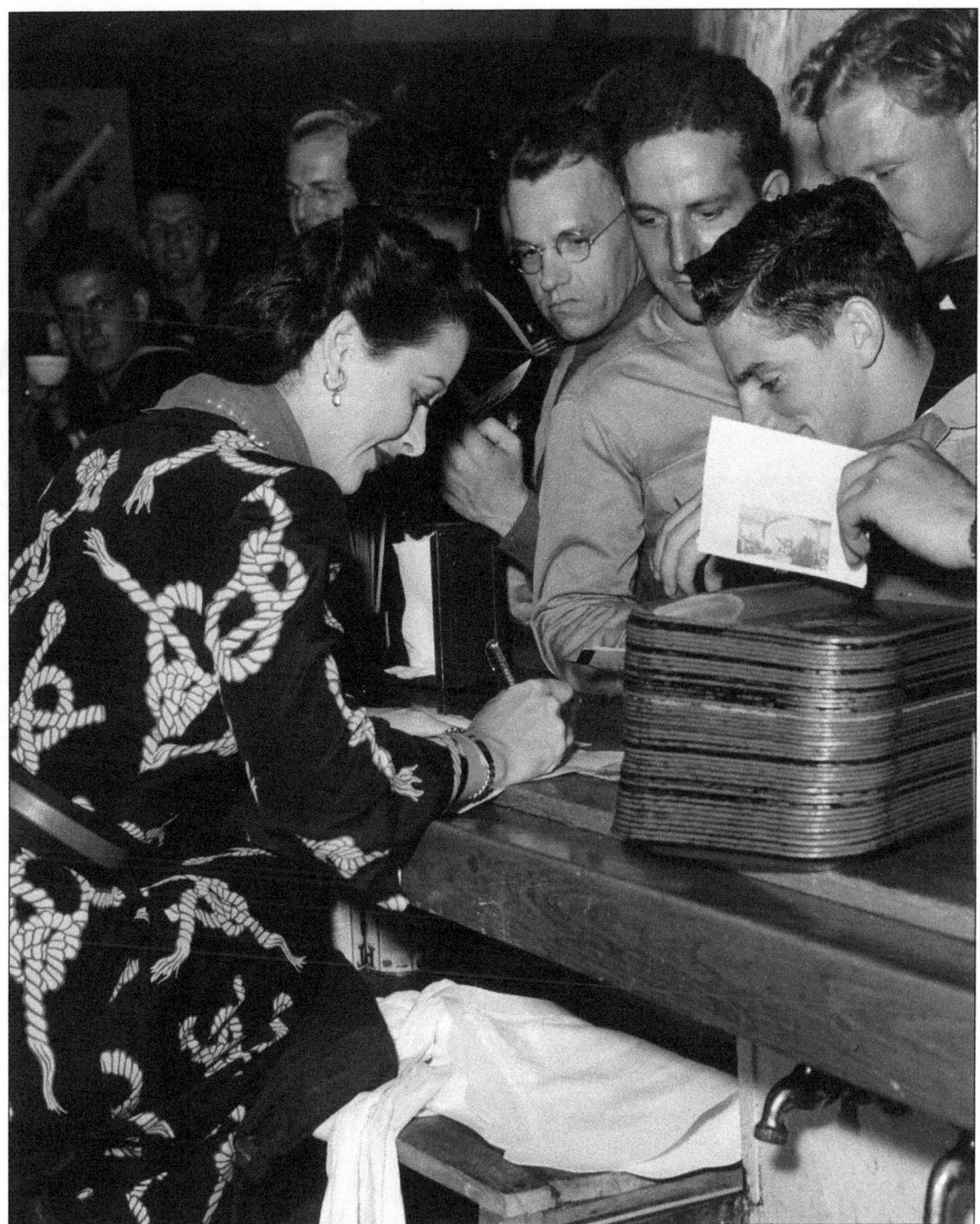

Between dancing and serving coffee and sandwiches, Hedy Lamarr always took a moment to sign one more autograph.

CHAPTER 11
THE GREATEST SHOW IN TOWN

The Andrews Sisters' unique harmony was a definitive sound for the war years.

"It would be impossible to walk into the Canteen and not be impressed," remembers producer A.C. Lyles, who went there as often as he could when he was in the Air Force. Of course, every serviceman who visited the Canteen could have said that, but the comment carried extra weight coming from A.C. Lyles.

Lyles, who started his career at Paramount in 1928, was working in the studio's Publicity Department when he joined the service. By the time he arrived at the Canteen in uniform — "I'd go there and see all my friends" — he had been around some of the biggest celebrities in Hollywood for years, and had been on close terms with many of them. And if this Hollywood habitué was impressed by the Canteen, he was particularly so when it came to the floor shows. "The big stars you'd see [performing] at the Mocambo and Ciro's and the Cocoanut Grove never could equal what was going on at the Canteen."[1]

Over the course of its three years, the Hollywood Canteen entertained millions of servicemen with the best singers, dancers, actors, actresses, comedians and radio personalities in show business.

Such singers as Ginny Simms, Jane Powell, Martha Tilton, Deanna Durbin, Jeanette MacDonald, Patricia Morrison, Frances Langford, Dinah Shore, Frank Sinatra, Dennis Morgan and Judy Garland wowed the boys whenever they appeared. Betty Hutton ("Murder, He Says"), Roy Rogers ("Don't Fence Me In") and the Andrews Sisters ("Boogie Woogie Bugle Boy") kept things lively. In her distinctive style, Lena Horne enthralled everyone with hits like "Stormy Weather," "Don't Get Around Much Anymore" and "Honeysuckle Rose." When she wasn't

Scores of servicemen line up to enter the Canteen for its Sunday afternoon concert.

overseas herself, Marlene Dietrich was up on that Canteen stage as often as possible. Her low-pitched, seductive, "Hello, boys," was always greeted by boisterous cheers and whistles that subsided only to hear Dietrich render such signature songs as "Boys In The Back Room" and the rousing "Lili Marlene."

It wasn't only the outstanding performers which made the Canteen shows so popular; it was also the variety of the entertainment. For hundreds of servicemen coming from all sorts of backgrounds, each with his own tastes and preferences, there was a diverse array of singers to please them — as it was with the footwork styles and distinctive personalities of dancers like Fay McKenzie, Ann Miller, Ted Lewis, Ray Bolger, Bill Robinson, the Nicholas Brothers, Joan McCracken, Veloz and Yolanda, and the NTG girls from the Florentine Gardens nightclub.

And there was no more sure-fire way to relax a young Marine, or to cheer up a homesick sailor, than with the Canteen's eclectic roster of comedians. Just a sampling included Bob Hope, Eddie Cantor, Joe E. Brown, George Burns and Gracie Allen, and Ken Murray and Marie Wilson. The Canteen had the perfect audience for Abbott and Costello's "Who's On First?" sketch, and Edgar Bergen and Charlie McCarthy's act where little Charlie would sigh as he ogled all the beautiful starlets around him. Servicemen also got huge kicks out of Danny Kaye, Phil Silvers, Jack Carson, and Red Skelton.

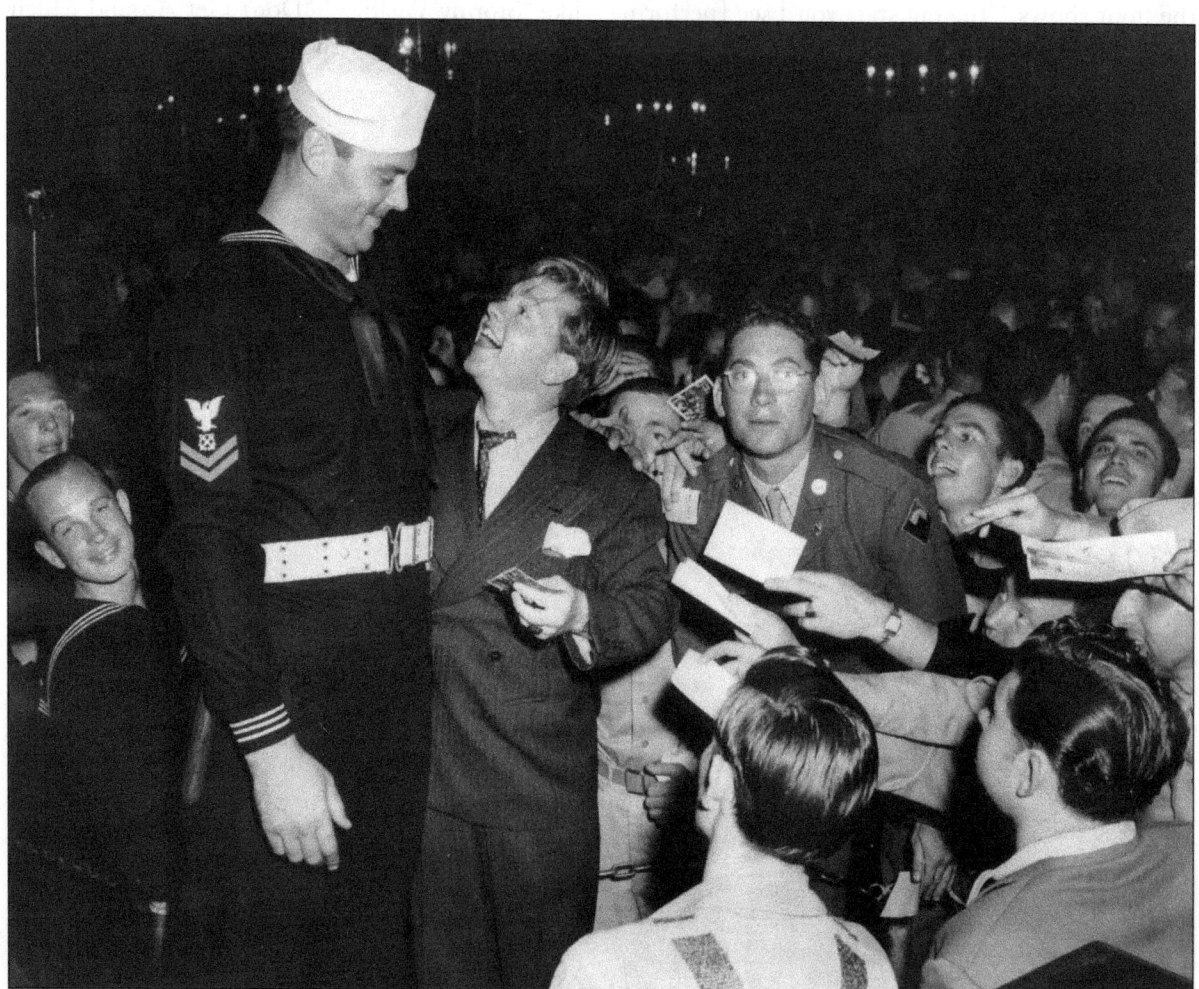

Two Mickeys! At six-foot five, Shore Patrolman Mickey Simpson looks down at Mickey Rooney during an autograph session.

The boys were so crazy about Skelton that Red would have to wait several minutes until all the whistling, whooping and clapping died down before he could start performing. The most requested routine was his "Guzzler's Gin" bit in which he pretended to be a radio pitchman who gets increasingly blotto — choking, sputtering, going cross-eyed — as he continued to drink the noxious liquor.

Among the Canteen's hundreds of entertainers, many defied neat categorization — George Jessel, gossip columnists Hedda Hopper and Louella Parsons — and there were multiple crossovers. Eddie Cantor, who was one of the Canteen's most frequent Masters of Ceremonies, also sang his trademark songs like "Makin' Whoopee," "Ida, Sweet As Apple Cider," and "Ma, He's Making Eyes At Me." Actors and actresses such as Marsha Hunt, George Raft, Rita Hayworth, Lana Turner, Rosalind Russell and Olivia de Havilland sang or danced or did shtick with the comedians — or, like Mickey Rooney, played drums with the bands. Actors, like Spencer Tracy, Cary Grant, Orson Welles, and Walter Pidgeon would stand on the stage and just talk with the boys.

There were at least two floor shows a night, one for each shift of volunteers, that lasted approximately 45 minutes. Some people nabbed tables, but the larger mass of soldiers, hostesses, and other volunteers sat down on the dance floor or stood along the perimeter of the room, relishing Hollywood's cream of the crop entertainers. Other onlookers included the patrons at the Angels' Tables on a

As Eddie Cantor acts as quiz master, The Quiz Kids answer questions from members of the audience.

raised dais in the rear corner, and the officers up in their small room on the second floor.

Most publicity about the Canteen's shows focused on the big name stars, but with so many hours a week to fill, there were ample opportunities for talented, up-and-coming performers to also give their all. While the majority of shows were booked days, even weeks, in advance, there were plenty of impromptu appearances by celebrity hostesses, busboys or kitchen staff who would be called up to the stage. This spontaneity only added to the Canteen's friendly, informal atmosphere — and made the soldiers feel that they were getting in on unique unrehearsed moments, happening just that night, just for them.

Servicemen visiting the Canteen on a February night in 1943 got a special treat after bandleader Kay Kyser spotted Charles Laughton among the volunteers. When he asked the great actor to come up to the stage, Laughton said, "I'm no singer or comedian, so I can't entertain you, much as I would like to." Then a soldier yelled out, "Give us 'The Gettysburg Address'!" and others picked up the cry. Then, amidst complete silence, Laughton delivered Lincoln's historic speech. When he finished, there was thunderous applause from everyone — and the wiping of tears from hundreds of eyes. Most of the time it had been jokes, snappy songs and swinging music — whatever kept thoughts of war at bay — that got the biggest hands. Yet that serious moment would never be forgotten. From then on, Laughton often interrupted his busboy duties to repeat his soul-stirring interpretation of the Gettysburg Address.[2]

A favorite, somewhat offbeat, personality who would leave the floor for the stage was Charles

Captivating Lena Horne was a favorite at the Canteen.

"Mickey" Simpson of the Shore Patrol. As did the Hollywood community itself, the Canteen had its own police station. There were tables specifically assigned to the Military Police (MP) and the Shore Patrol (SP) that were placed on either side of the entrance to the main room. In addition to preventing any outbreaks of trouble, these "police" were walking information bureaus.

Simpson was the most popular — and recognizable — Shore Patrolman. A heavyweight boxing champion in New York in 1935, and a former bodyguard for Claudette Colbert, the six foot, five inches tall, 230 pound Simpson began getting small roles in movies in the late 1930s, including one in John Ford's *Stagecoach* (1939). During the war, he joined the Navy and became a Shore Patrolman assigned to the Canteen. He greeted servicemen, gave out his autograph, and from time to time, was called up on the stage to kibbitz with some of the performing celebrities.

After the war, Simpson resumed his acting career, usually playing bad guys in Westerns. Over the next twenty-five years, Mickey appeared in more than 140 films, including *She Wore A Yellow Ribbon* (1949), *Giant* (1956), and *The Greatest Story Ever Told* (1965).

One of the extemporaneous parts of the entertainment that never failed to tickle the young men was when they were called on themselves. As a soldier or sailor joined the professionals on stage in some embarrassing skits — wearing a hula skirt, murdering a song, a joke, a dance — his buddies in the audience howled with laughter.

Young men in uniform especially resonated to the performers and music with which they were familiar.

Rudy Vallee's Coast Guard Band frequently played at the Canteen.

Bob Hope was undoubtedly one of the Canteen's most frequent and popular entertainers.

When hostess Jean Porter wasn't dancing with the boys or serving them food, she was singing to them as part of the floor shows. She may not have been the biggest star at the Canteen, but the servicemen were crazy about her because they knew her and her songs from the "soundies." These were film jukebox presentations that were popular in the early forties where a fellow could plunk a nickel down and watch a three-minute musical short on a 24-inch plastic screen. Porter, a perky MGM actress-singer-dancer, was featured in many soundies and the minute she stepped onto the Canteen stage, the soldiers would call out the names of her songs they wanted to hear. "Their favorite was 'Rum and Coca Cola'" [3]

Servicemen were always aware of what was going on in the entertainment world by way of the Armed Forces Radio Services (AFRS). Certainly they were kept up to date on all the big band sounds — the very ones they would enjoy when they came to the Canteen. In her commentary for the biography, *Mother Goddam*, Bette Davis said, "I think the greatest contributions of any union to the entertainment for the servicemen in our Canteen was the musicians unions. Without music for dancing, we would have had no Canteen. We could not possibly have afforded to pay musicians — we never had to –plus all our servicemen heard all the great bands of the day." [4]

Over the Canteen's three-year existence, more than four hundred bands delighted countless servicemen. Some of the most popular included those of Freddy Martin, Tommy and Jimmy Dorsey, Duke Ellington, Carmen Cavallero, Spike Jones, Ted Fio Rito, Gene Krupa, Horace Heidt, Louis Armstrong, Benny Goodman, Harry James and Kay Kyser. Kyser and his band were the most regular, playing nearly every Saturday night, even if it meant having to fly in to Hollywood from his other gigs around the country. Kyser, who was in charge of the Canteen's musical activities, was well-known for appearing in more than half a dozen films and for his radio show, "Kay Kyser's Kollege of Musical Knowledge," that drew 20 million listeners a week.

During the 1940s, many celebrities had their own radio programs and, thanks to the proximity of the radio studios to Cahuenga Boulevard, were able to broadcast a number of them from the Hollywood Canteen. Eddie Cantor sometimes brought his show over from NBC at Sunset and Vine. Red Skelton, also from NBC, frequently kept the guys in stitches as he became Junior, the Mean Widdle Kid ("I dood it!"), Clem Kadiddlehopper or Willy Lump Lump.

CBS allowed Ken Murray — who produced and starred, with Marie Wilson, in Ken Murray's Blackouts at the El Capitan Theater on Vine Street — to broadcast his variety show at the Canteen. Several other radio programs occasionally followed suit with such stars as Frank Sinatra, Claudette Colbert, Jack Benny, Burns and Allen, Leopold Stokowski, Betty Hutton, Dinah Shore, and the Canteen's own Bette Davis.

Bob Hope jumped right in to do his Tuesday night broadcast from the Canteen on October 13, 1942 — just ten days after the Canteen opened. The rapport that Hope had with servicemen — which would be life-long — really clicked at the Canteen. He regaled the boys with his self-deprecating humor, racy cracks about beautiful girls and his putting down of officers.

"…Here I am doing the first broadcast from the Hollywood Canteen," Hope began. "This really is a marvelous place. Any enlisted man can come here. Be entertained by the top Hollywood talent. Get free food served by Hollywood beauties. Dance with girls like Hedy Lamarr or Lana Turner. And then go back to camp and be used to heat the barracks."

And…

"The more important the celebrity is, the better job he gets. For instance, last night, Cary Grant was the host, Charles Boyer the waiter, Gary Cooper the hat check boy, and Jimmy Cagney the Master of Ceremonies. And everyone said I did a swell job taking care of the washroom." [5]

Though the Canteen was open seven days a week, Sundays were unique. The hours were from two in the afternoon till eight in the evening (instead of

Hollywood Canteen

Affiliated With American Theatre Wing, Inc.

HOLLYWOOD, CALIFORNIA

OFFICERS
PRESIDENT—Bette Davis
1ST VICE-PRES.—J. K. Wallace
2ND VICE-PRES.—John Garfield
3RD VICE-PRES.—Mervyn LeRoy
4TH VICE-PRES.—Carroll Hollister
5TH VICE-PRES.—Mrs. John Ford
EXEC. SECRETARY—Jean Lewin
TREASURER—Ray Marcus

COMMITTEE CHAIRMEN
BLDG. & ALTERATION—Alfred C. Ybarra
BUS. MGEM'T—Jules C. Stein
CHECKERS—Paul Jaffee
DECORATORS—Casey Roberts
ENTERTAINMENT:
  HON. CHAIRMAN, Bob Hope
  CHAIRMAN, Kay Kyser
  CELEBRITIES—Ann Warner
  RADIO—Georgia Fifield
  VARIETY ARTISTS—Florine Bale
HOSTESSES—Doris Stein, Florence C. Cadrez
HOSTS—Mervyn LeRoy, Harry Crocker
KITCHEN EQUIP.—William Simon
MAINTENANCE—Paul Doyle
MUSIC—John TeGroen, Baron Moorehead
OFFICERS OF THE DAY—Edwin H. Knopf
PUBLICITY—Mack Millar
SNACK BAR—Mrs. John Ford
STAGE MGEM'T—George Ramsey
TREASURERS—Catherine Baldwin

DIRECTOR OF FOOD—Chef Milani
LEGAL ADVISOR—Dudley R. Purse

SPONSORS OF HOLLYWOOD CANTEEN
Actors Equity Assn.
Affil. Property Craftsman, IATSE Local 44
Amer. Fed. of Musicians, Local 47
Amer. Fed. of Musicians, Local 767
Amer. Fed. of Radio Artists
Amer. Guild of Musical Artists
Amer. Guild of Variety Artists
Amer. Soc. of Composers, Authors and Publ.
Artists Managers Guild
Asso. Motion Pic. Cost., IATSE Local 705
Association of Motion Picture Producers
B.S.E.I.U., Local 99
C., L.&R.F.D., Local 1247
Federated Amusement & Allied Crafts
Film Technicians, IATSE Local 683
Independent Publicists
Int. Photographers, IATSE Local 659
Int. Sound Tech., IATSE Local 695
Makeup Artists, IATSE Local 706
Mot. Pic. Hair Stylists, IATSE Local 706
Motion Picture Illustrators
M.P. Set Electricians, IATSE Local 728
M.P. Studio Grips, IATSE Local 80
M.P. Studio Projec., IATSE Local 165
M.P. Painters & Scenic Art., Local 644
Radio Writers Guild
Screen Cartoonists Guild
Screen Directors Guild
Screen Office Employees Guild
Screen Publicists Guild
Screen Readers Guild
Screen Set Designers
Screen Writers Guild
Society of Motion Picture Art Directors
Society of Motion Picture Film Editors
Society of Motion Picture Int. Decorators
Songwriters Protective Assn.
Studio Carpenters, Local 946
Studio Elec. Union, IBEW Local 40
Studio L. & U. Workers, IATSE Local 727
Studio Misc. Employees, Local 1104
Studio Trans. Drivers Union, Local 399
Studio Util. Emp. Union, Local 724
U.A.J.P.&S., Local 78
W.C.U.,B.S.E., Local 101

ENDORSED BY
California State Federation of Labor
Hollywood Victory Committee
Hollywood Writers Mobilization
State Theatrical Fed. of California
U.S.O.

October 23, 1943

Mr. Bob Hope
10346 Moorpark Street
North Hollywood, California

Dear Bob Hope:

Please accept our gratitude for your graciousness in greeting our British guests at the Canteen recently.

The hospitality extended to these men by Hollywood, cannot help but indicate to them our genuine friendliness and appreciation.

The many words of pleasure and gratitude expressed by the British service men, prove to us that it was a really successful welcome which you helped us extend.

Our best wishes and our kindest regards.

Sincerely,

Bette Davis,
President

1451 NORTH CAHUENGA BOULEVARD   PHONE HEMPSTEAD 4801

Bette Davis wrote hundreds of letters of appreciation like this one to Bob Hope.

7:00 PM to midnight), and they were devoted to symphonic entertainment. Servicemen who might have jitterbugged to hot, fast music on a week night, loved the more classical concerts so much they jam-packed the place every Sunday.

The Canteen's own eighty-piece orchestra was under the batons of such world-renowned conductors as Leopold Stokowski and Otto Klemperer. Among the great pianists who played for the soldiers were José Iturbi and Arthur Rubenstein. The powerful baritone John Charles Thomas was a regular who lifted everybody's spirits when he sang his affecting rendition of "The Lord's Prayer" as well as other favorite songs. Many additional stars, including Jeanette MacDonald, Nelson Eddy, Gertrude Lawrence, Basil Rathbone, and ballet dancers Alicia Markova and Anton Dolin, often gave up their Sundays to entertain the enlisted men. The Sunday concerts were over around 5:30 PM, and the Canteen got back to business as usual. Servicemen were again eating, drinking, dancing with starlets, getting their autographs, and applauding the floor shows, till, after about two and a half hours, they headed back to their bases; the volunteers returned to their homes and families.

By day, by night — from Garland to Laughton, Skelton to Stokowski — the entertainers kept giving, and the servicemen kept talking about them after they left Hollywood for all points of war. News of the greatest show in town spread all over the world.

Nils Thor Granlund (NTG), who staged the shows at the Florentine Gardens nightclub, regularly sent his NTG girls to the Canteen. Here they dance with "kilted" servicemen.

Orson Welles performs in a live radio broadcast from the Canteen.

Ted Lewis does his famous "Me And My Shadow" routine accompanied by a singing trio.

The Canteen's audience always laughed at Danny Kaye's jokes and skits.

Red Skelton performing his famous Guzzler's Gin skit for the servicemen.

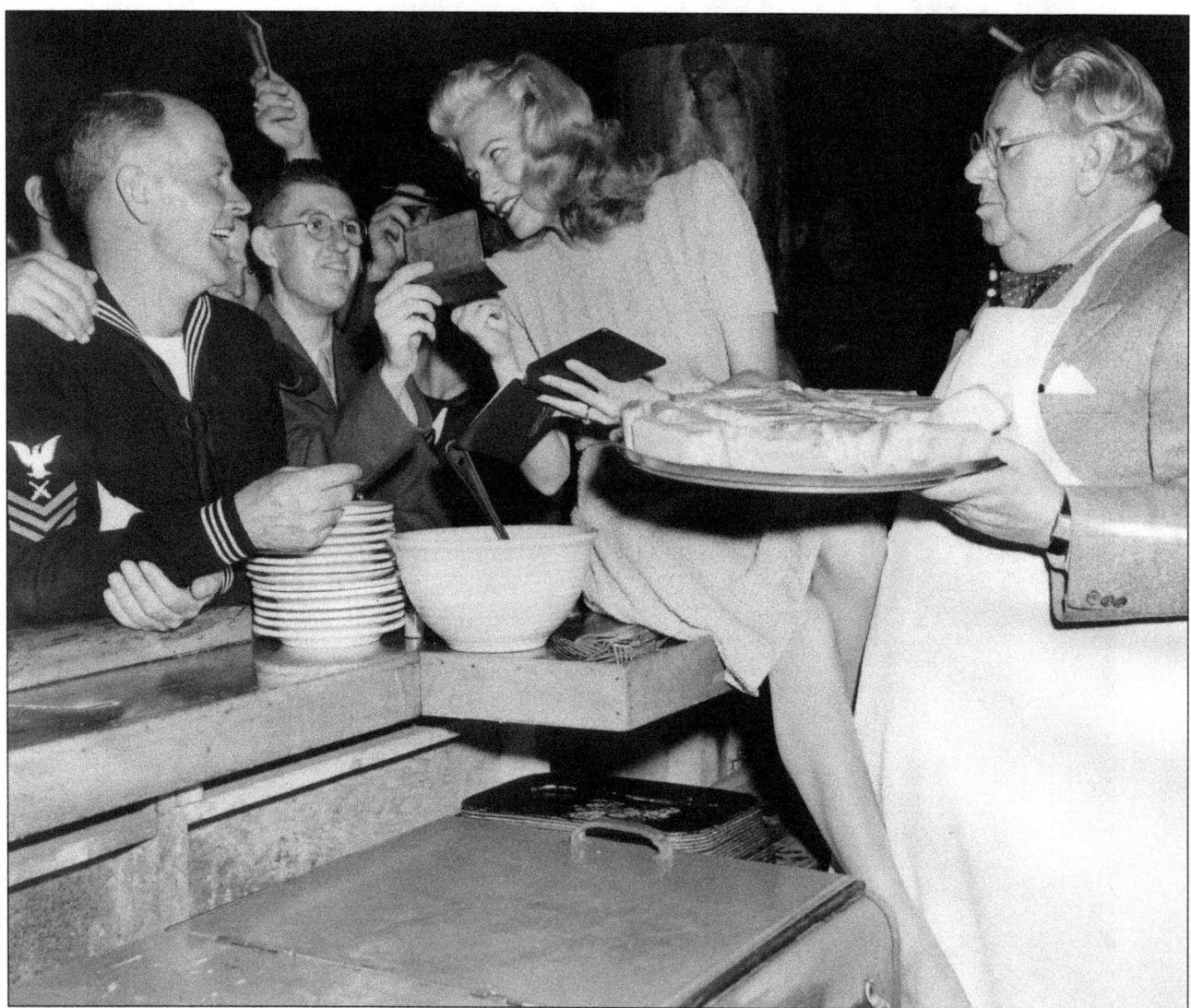
Actress Chili Williams flirts and signs autographs while S.Z. Sakall prepares to serve sandwiches.

Olivia de Havilland and Ken Murray laugh it up during a radio show broadcast from the Canteen's stage.

As co-founder Bette Davis looks on, Mary Pickford takes a bow at the Canteen's First Birthday party.

A regular entertainer at the Canteen, José Iturbi plays for a typical Sunday afternoon audience.

The always popular Deanna Durbin signs another autograph.

CHAPTER 12
SPECIAL ATTRACTIONS

Lana Turner, Deanna Durbin and Marlene Dietrich escort the Canteen's millionth serviceman, Sgt. Carl Bell, into the building.

Most servicemen who came to the Canteen for the first time had a general idea of what to expect, as they had heard about it from fellow soldiers and read about it in movie magazines. The bounty was well known: dancing with glamorous stars, free food, fabulous live music — and such general consistency was comforting. Yet there was nothing routine about the Canteen, and no night was ever the same as another.

In addition to the surprises inherent in mixtures of G.I.s, celebrities, pretty volunteers and varying entertainment, the Canteen offered unique events and specific celebrations.

Within a month of its opening, the Canteen was hosting almost 20,000 servicemen a week; in March, 1943, Seaman Wilham Rakowski of Chicago was feted as its 500,000th visitor. Granted a modern day Aladdin's lamp, Rakowski wished for a two-day pass to visit a movie studio. Immediately, a telegram was sent to his Commanding Officer with an invitation for him to come to Warner Bros. — home studio of Bette Davis and many other dedicated stars of the Canteen.

On September 15, 1943, just a few weeks before its first birthday, the Canteen created an extravagant welcome for the arrival of its one-millionth uniformed guest. When Sergeant William E. W. Bell of Rising Star, Texas, walked through the doors, he stepped into the spotlight where the amazed young man's arms were suddenly filled with expensive presents given by an honor guard of Marlene Dietrich, Lana Turner, and Deanna Durbin. Sergeant Bell, a member of an Army Company of Engineers, was overjoyed with his gifts, some of which included a gold wristwatch, a wardrobe suitcase, a toiletries case, a gift certificate for merchandise and a wallet. Everyone was treated to a huge cake that took Chef Milani two days to prepare. (The Millionth Man saga would later be fictionalized in the 1944 Warner Bros. movie, *Hollywood Canteen*.) Such timely celebrations could reward only one man, but the Canteen had another way of extending the possibilities for prizes. Twice every night, drawings were held to give lucky servicemen twenty-five dollar war bonds donated by the studios.

Another big party during the first year wasn't for servicemen, though a handful of them had been invited. On Labor Day, 1943, many volunteers who had worked so hard over such long hours to make the Canteen a success took off for a picnic at Barney Oldfield's Country Club in Van Nuys. More than a thousand members of Hollywood's entertainment industry — artists, dancers, musicians, secretaries, writers, hairstylists, electricians, agents, publicists,

The Canteen's millionth visiting serviceman, Sgt. Carl Bell, receives a greeting kiss from Betty Grable.

stars and starlets of film and radio — got together with their families and friends to drink free beer, eat the sandwiches they brought, and enjoy each others' company.

Wearing bright-colored slacks, sweaters, and peasant dresses, such favorites as Lynn Bari, Ginny Simms, Patricia Morrison, Marsha Hunt, Heather Angel, Joan Leslie, Jean Porter and Ruth Hussey listened to professional M.C.s over loud-speakers keep things moving every minute, from noon until six in the evening.

The millionth serviceman to visit the Canteen, Sgt. Carl Bell, is serenaded by Jimmy Durante.

Organized play included swimming, scooter races, potato sack races, a dance contest, and two baseball games. The highlight of the afternoon was when the "Civies," Eddie Cantor's baseball team, defeated Shore Patrolman Mickey Simpson's "Draftees" by a score of seven to six. Among those on the winning team were John Garfield, Eddie Bracken, Joe E. Brown, Buster Keaton, Johnny Johnson, Rod Cameron, Hoagy Carmichael and Walter Wolff King. Freddy Martin and Chuck Faulkner provided the day's music, and when "The Star-Spangled Banner" was played at six PM, the picnic ended. A number of the guests then drove back to the Canteen to help greet the servicemen who began arriving at seven.

Barney Oldfield's Country Club was also the site of the 1944 volunteer picnic, but in 1945, the event was an old-fashioned barn dance held at the Paddock Club on Riverside Drive in Burbank. In her invitation to the thousands of Canteen volunteers, Bette wrote, "wear your dungarees, gingham, Stetsons, or what have you."[1]

Servicemen were definitely present at the Canteen's First Birthday party. Held on October 31st, 1943 (though the official birthday was October 3rd), the celebration offered scores of stars as hosts and hostesses to thousands of soldiers. Bette Davis and John Garfield introduced such guests as baritone John Charles Thomas, who served as Master of Ceremonies and also sang "The Lord's

Left to right: Deanna Durbin, Joan Leslie, Lana Turner and K.T. Stevens during the celebration for Sgt. Carl Bell as the Canteen's millionth visitor.

Prayer." Renowned symphony conductor, Leopold Stokowski, directed the Hollywood Canteen's 80-piece orchestra for a nationwide radio broadcast. Among other celebrities who entertained during the evening were Bob Hope, Marlene Dietrich, Joan Leslie, Mary Pickford, Olivia de Havilland, Patricia Morrison, Mary Brian, Jane Wyman, Captain Ronald Reagan, Ginny Simms, Frances Langford, Kay Kyser and Eddie Cantor.

Major William Wyler, an Academy Award-winning director (*Mrs. Miniver*, 1942), who went to England with the Eighth Air Force, presented the Canteen with a huge service flag bearing 6254 stars for "the guys from the motion picture industry who are out there fighting for us." [2] Canteen director, Mervyn LeRoy, also a versatile film director (*Waterloo Bridge*, 1940; *Madame Curie*, 1943), revealed a Hall of Honor. Located in the entry area, the Hall of Honor was a wall of photographs showing uniformed actors and others from the movie industry serving in the Armed Forces. Some of the men represented were Captain Clark Gable, Captain Ronald Reagan and Lieutenant James Stewart, all of the Army Air Corps; U.S. Naval flight instructor, Lieutenant Commander Robert Taylor, and U.S. Coast Guard Chief Petty Officer, Victor Mature.

Chef Milani wheeled in another of his colossal cakes that Bette Davis cut into thousands of small pieces to satisfy everyone who was there. Bette then introduced thirteen war heroes: Captain Jack Landers, Sergeant Bill Haynes, Corporal Keith Thompson, Private Taylor Barnes, Private John Zdiriencik, Lieutenant Howard Burrett, all of the

Co-founders John Garfield and Bette Davis cut a small cake during the Canteen's First Birthday party.

Army; Lieutenant (j.g.) William Masoner of the Navy; Colonel William J. Fox, Captain Albert L. Clark and Captain K.M. Ford, of the Marine Corps, and Boatswain's First Mate First Class Lawrence Peterson of the Coast Guard.

The *Los Angeles Times* caught the essence of the First Birthday in a story that ran the next day: "There was laughter. And tears. It was stupendous. But all the clamor and glamour at yesterday's party were for one man. He wore a khaki uniform and his cap was folded in his belt. Or he was in blue with a white cap stuffed in the top of his bell-bottomed pants. There have been 1,100,000 just like him who have been entertained at the Canteen since it opened just a year ago. It was his party yesterday…He sure had himself a great time. And sometime today, he's going to sit down and write Mom about it."[3]

Bette Davis, John Garfield and other Canteen stalwarts knew that of all parties, those for Thanksgiving and Christmas would be the most important. The volunteers went all out to become surrogate families for the many servicemen who would not be home for the holidays. To accommodate the thousands of soldiers who showed up at both events, the Canteen opened its doors at two in the afternoon and closed at midnight.

Thanksgiving, 1942, was the first time the Canteen provided turkey dinners — carved from over seventy large turkeys — with all the trimmings. The following two Thanksgivings broke the previous records, both for attendance and for the number of turkeys served. The 1945 Thanksgiving was especially memorable, as it would also mark the Canteen's final day of operation. Long before the two o'clock opening, the line of servicemen extended for more than a block down Cahuenga Boulevard. With so many young men aching to get in, the volunteers had to clear out the Canteen every hour to make room for another waiting group.

The Christmas parties of 1942, 1943, and 1944 were spectacular. Volunteers filled the Canteen with beautiful decorations and trimmed a huge tree, under which they placed sacks of presents. As with Thanksgiving, soldiers were admitted in hourly shifts to let as many guests as possible get in on the fun.

Eddie Cantor, dressed as Santa Claus, was the M.C. for all three years. Bette Davis and John Garfield joined Cantor on stage with such stars as Dorothy Lamour, Ann Miller, Betty Grable, and Linda Darnell to toss miniature duffel bags filled with gifts out to happy servicemen. The boys were thrilled with entertainment by the likes of Burns

Husband and wife, Ronald Reagan and Jane Wyman, arrive for the Canteen's First Birthday party.

and Allen, José Iturbi, Lena Horne, and several top orchestras which played till midnight. Celebrities, from Spencer Tracy and Charles Coburn to Paulettle Goddard and Olivia de Havilland, served over 5,000 ham and turkey dinners at each of the yearly parties; they performed skits, danced with the soldiers, and sang Christmas carols. The year that Bing Crosby sang them with his young sons, "there was not a dry eye in the Canteen."[4]

Parties may have been special attractions, but they were not the only kinds. The Canteen played cupid to any number of couples, and there were at least six celebrities whose romances were sparked during their times as volunteers.

Though Betty Grable and Harry James had met before, it was "at the Canteen...that the two really got to know each other," which led to their elopement in 1943.[5] While serving at the Canteen, Susan Hayward connected with Jess Barker and married him in 1944. Hedy Lamarr was in the kitchen about to wash piles of dishes when Bette Davis introduced her to the man who would be drying them — John Loder. As Lamarr put it, "[a]nd the Canteen, of all places, is where I met my third husband."[6] Two months later at the Christmas party, Lamarr realized that she would forsake all others for Loder. After they were married, both Loders continued to volunteer. When the Canteen hosted the visiting British Aviation Aircraft Unit in October, 1943, "Bob Hope and Hedy Lamarr did an ad lib routine which Hope started with, 'Hedy, your husband is working in the kitchen. What about us cooking here?'"[7]

The Canteen could also be a matchmaker when it came to careers. Janis Paige, who was born Donna May Tjaden, had arrived in Hollywood from Tacoma, Washington, hoping to become an opera star. Her mother was volunteering at the Canteen and persuaded someone on the entertainment committee to let her daughter sing for the soldiers. After a little coaxing from mom, Janis got up on the stage and sang some arias. The audience loved her. So did Ida Koverman, who was also volunteering that night. Ida worked at M.G.M. and had the ear of Louis B. Mayer. She arranged for Janis to meet

A galaxy of stars listen to speeches during the Canteen's First Birthday party. (L to R) Mervin LeRoy, Kay Kyser, John Garfield, Gracie Allen, George Burns, Bob Hope and Jane Wyman.

with Mayer, who signed her to a seven-year contract. A year or so later, M.G.M. released her and she was immediately picked up by Warner Bros. where she won the role of Angela in *Hollywood Canteen*. The zestful redhead's career skyrocketed, and over the following fifty years, Janis Paige became a star of movies, stage (most memorably of the 1954 smash Broadway musical, *The Pajama Game*), and television.

You just never knew who would be at the Canteen, or what some contacts, such as Paige's with Koverman, might lead to. Unfortunately, there was one chance meeting that did not have a happy ending.

Gene Tierney was one of the most gorgeous actresses in pictures — even by Hollywood standards. Her "[e]xquisitely etched cheekbones, slanted blue-green eyes and an exotic feline beauty"[8] would make her unforgettable in such films as *Laura* (1944) and *Leave Her to Heaven* (1945).

According to her autobiography, Tierney, who was married to designer, Oleg Cassini, was glad to volunteer at the Canteen and showed up one night during the first month of a pregnancy. A few days after that evening, her face was covered with red spots. "The doctor diagnosed my problem as German measles," Tierney wrote, "something called rubella, and told me it would only last a week...Little was known then about the connections between German measles in early pregnancy and the damage to an unborn child's nervous system."[9]

After their daughter, Daria, was born, Tierney and Cassini learned that the baby was "hopelessly retarded," as well as deaf, with visual impairment. Eventually, Daria was put in a special home and the Cassinis divorced.

About a year after Daria's birth, Tierney was at a tennis party when a young woman came up and introduced herself. She was in the women's branch of the Marines, and had met Tierney, she said, at the Canteen. Then she asked, "'Did you happen to catch the German measles after that night?' I looked at her," Tierney wrote, "too stunned to speak." It turned out that the woman had left her camp where there was an outbreak of German measles. "'I broke quarantine to come to the Canteen to meet the stars. Everyone told me I shouldn't, but I just had to go. And you were my favorite.'"

Tierney did not say anything "of the tragedy that had occurred." But, she wrote, after that, she did not care if she "was ever again anyone's favorite actress.

Raffle tickets for $25 War Bonds and various prizes were donated each night by major movie studios.

"I have long since stopped blaming the lady Marine...for what happened to us. But Daria was, of course, a war baby, born in 1943...Daria was my war effort."[10]

There was indeed remarkable dedication of so many movie stars and top-drawer entertainers, and, understandably, theirs were the names publicized; the ones talked about. They were part of every special attraction, and sometimes, of the Canteen's special features, too, such as writing letters for soldiers.

When a celebrity wrote to a serviceman's mother, it was a double treat for him, knowing that his family back home could also be meeting the star he met in Hollywood. Carmel Myers, a popular actress in silent films, had a pet project of watching for boys in the uniforms of our Allies. After getting the names and addresses of their families, Carmel would spend the following day writing to a mother or a wife across the sea.

Of course, the nightly letter-writing service was overwhelmingly done by members of the Screen Office Employees Guild — who had a small sign on their desk saying, "Dictate your letter to a real studio secretary." By the end of the evening, forty or fifty letters had been dictated, typed and mailed. Postcards with photographs of the Canteen were handed out so the servicemen could show the folks back home where they had been having such a wonderful time.

Other unique features that the Canteen offered were also conducted by the studios' behind-the-scenes people whose names might not be recognized outside of Hollywood. One such activity was the sketching of soldiers and sailors by studio cartoonists like Don Barclay who presented his amused subjects with autographed caricatures of themselves.

At least three of the Westmore brothers — they of the famous makeup dynasty — delighted the servicemen and women by putting on makeup shows. One night, Perc Westmore, who volunteered more than the rest of his clan, changed Mickey Rooney into a miniature Clark Gable, and Bette Davis into Bela Lugosi as Dracula. Bette, who was always willing to be unglamorous on screen, was delighted by her transformation. For Bette as Bela could bring riotous laughter from the Canteen crowd — her favorite audience of all.

John Garfield, Bette Davis and famed conductor Leopold Stokowski are on stage for the Canteen's First Birthday party.

Many special guests were seated on the raised dais, usually reserved for the Angels' Tables, to observe the Canteen's First Birthday party.

Leopold Stokowski conducts an 80-piece orchestra during the Canteen's First Birthday party.

With assistance from actor Jack LaRue (in chef's clothes), Bette Davis and Spencer Tracy prepare to carve a Thanksgiving turkey.

Ann Miller and Linda Darnell were two of the many stars who handed out thousands of presents on Christmas Day in 1943.

On Christmas Eve, 1944, Benita Hume (Mrs. Ronald Coleman), unknown, Ronald Coleman, unknown, Herbert Marshall and set designer Harry Reif hand gifts to grateful servicemen.

Left to right: Doris Kenyon, Mary Ford, Eddie Cantor, Sybil Brand and Cobina Wright wrap Christmas presents to be given away at the Canteen.

While Betty Grable gets ready to hang Christmas decorations, Bette Davis helps Eddie Cantor become Santa Claus.

Martha O'Driscoll chats with a sailor who just won a $25 War Bond during the nightly raffle.

As Bob Hope and Marlene Dietrich look on, Bette Davis points to Captain Clark Gable's photograph hanging on the Canteen's Hall of Honor.

To celebrate Joan Leslie's birthday, Chef Milani baked a large cake for her to cut and hand to her fans.

Three soldiers are called up on stage to sing with Irene Manning.

Skits were a common feature at the Canteen. Here, Bette Davis and make-up artist Perc Westmore dress a visiting soldier in women's clothes.

CHAPTER 13
A PLACE TO STAY: THE HOLLYWOOD GUILD AND CANTEEN

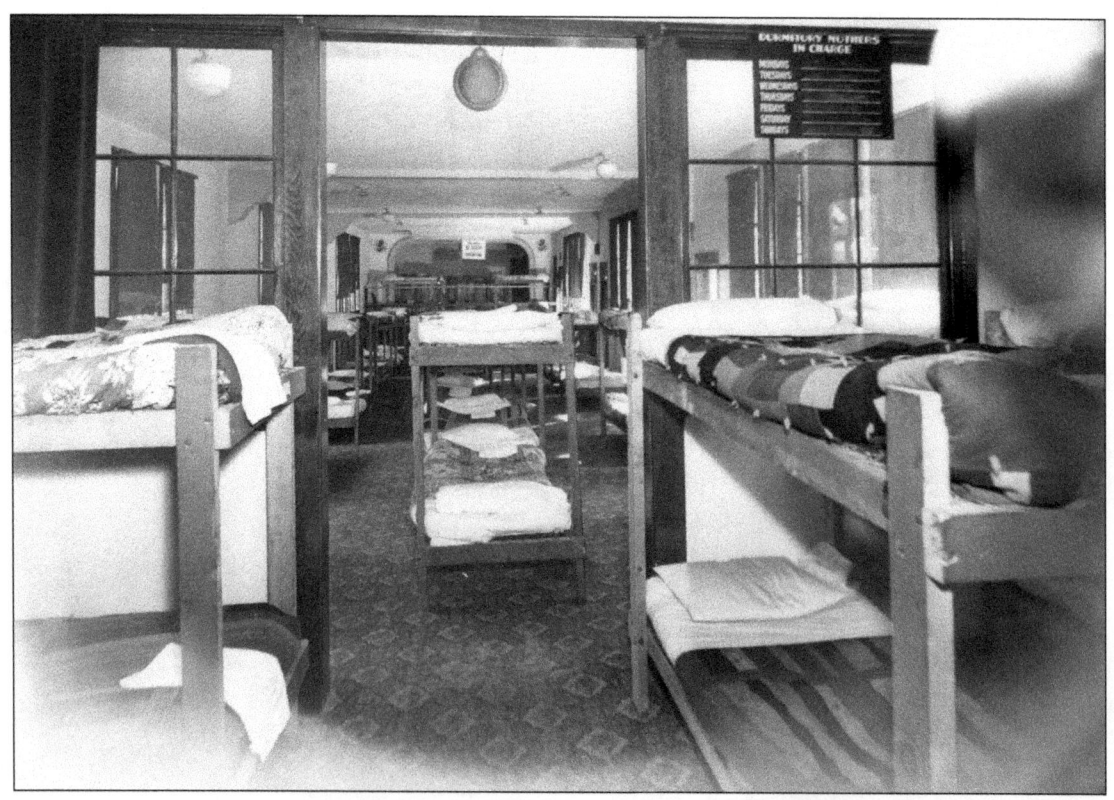

The Hollywood Guild and Canteen housed hundreds of servicemen each night.

If Hollywood wasn't where all the thousands of servicemen stationed in or passing through Southern California converged, it certainly looked like it. Throughout the war, members of the Armed Forces were drawn to the town that was more than a town; to the mecca of entertainment where the bright lights, hot spots and pretty girls were; where theatres stayed open around the clock, and the Hollywood Canteen was the biggest draw of all.

On the weekends, soldiers outnumbered civilians ten to one in the streets of downtown Hollywood. Many wound up sleeping in cars, on park benches, or in the aisles and lobbies of theatres. As the Hollywood community became aware of these overcrowded conditions, venues of hospitality opened up. Dormitories and auditoriums in schools and churches were made available; young men in uniform were welcomed into residents' own bedrooms. California's theatre owners collected $190,000 from audiences in a "Beds for Buddies" campaign to match whatever funds the state of California contributed. Though these were good stop-gap measures, something was needed beyond securing scattered accommodations.

Enter Mrs. Abraham Lehr, and the special house she provided.

Anne Neill Lehr had been in charge of a small charitable organization through which she helped needy people in the movie industry. As part of her outreach, she rented a large house to shelter

Surrounded by many of "her boys", Anne "Mom" Lehr founded the Hollywood Guild and Canteen, which provided beds and meals for soldiers while on leave in Hollywood.

Hollywood's broken-down stuntmen, unemployed actors and underfed extras. But after the attacks on Pearl Harbor, Anne's focus changed. Many of her guests had taken jobs in war plants; soon the roomy house was nearly empty.

The house itself had once belonged to silent screen star Dustin Farnum, which gave it a unique place in Hollywood history. Farnum had starred in Cecil B. DeMille's *The Squaw Man* (1914), which was the first feature length motion picture made in Hollywood. *The Squaw Man*, with its varied Southern California scenery and compelling drama, became such a commercial success that it drew film companies away from New York — the main site of early film production — and helped establish Hollywood as the movie capital of the world.

On May 15, 1942, Anne opened the doors of the Farnum mansion as a free hotel for servicemen and called it the Hollywood Guild and Canteen. Located at 1284 North Crescent Heights Boulevard, Mrs. Lehr's place would become the closest thing to home for soldiers on a furlough.

Because Anne had neglected to publicize the Guild, she had to send some of her assistants to drive around Hollywood and personally invite the enlisted men they found to the new sanctuary. Some were skeptical, but others took a chance, till about fifty young men came to the house and devoured a delicious turkey dinner. After a restful night's sleep and a hearty breakfast the next morning, the boys left satisfied and happy.

The good word spread about "Mom's" — as the Guild quickly became known — not only through the streets of Hollywood, but through every country to which the soldiers traveled. *Liberty* magazine cited one example: a few incapacitated Allied prisoners in

Left to right: Jane Russell, Toni Stevens and Martha Tilton sign "pin-up" photos for the boys.

a German camp were being exchanged and leaving for home. "One of them was an Australian infantryman, his face scarred by a shrapnel wound. As he packed his few belongings, an American flier sidled up and slipped him a piece of paper saying, 'Pal, if you ever get to the States, here's a place for you to stay.' The Australian opened the paper and on it was scrawled: '1284 North Crescent Heights Boulevard, Hollywood, California. Ask for Mom.'"[1]

As a gift from Tom Breneman and his popular radio show, *Breakfast in Hollywood*, a $10,000 swimming pool was installed on the grounds. In addition to the large main house, new structures were raised (with the muscle of the Seabees assigned from the base at Port Hueneme) and nearby existing buildings were put into use. Soon what Anne had started with 30 cots became an operation of hundreds of beds, with more in an abandoned market a block away. A private house one street over became home to another 100 or so men on leave. The Guild was able to sleep an average of 800 men a night, with as many as 1200 on weekends. (About a hundred servicewomen were cared for in a house not far from the Guild; officers stayed at their own club at 6700 Sunset Boulevard.)

Lehr offered clean, comfortable beds and three square meals — plus plenty of snacks at any hour. The boys drank $100 worth of milk a day and could eat as many as 1400 eggs at each breakfast. Ping pong tables, radios, phonographs with all the latest records, a jukebox for dance music, tickets for theatres, sporting events and radio shows were all available at the Guild. The very neighborhood could seem entertaining to young men in Hollywood for the first time. Up the street on Crescent Heights at Sunset Boulevard was the glamorous Garden of Allah apartment hotel — favored by such actors as Errol Flynn and Orson Welles — and Schwab's Drug Store, a noted movie-star hangout (where it would be depicted as Hollywood's "Headquarters" in Billy Wilder's *Sunset Boulevard*, 1950).

The Guild's guests were encouraged to come and go at will and stay as long as they pleased. They had complete run of the place, which they were glad to help care for. Anne Lehr wanted the fighting men to feel comfortable under her roof. She told *Liberty* magazine, "Whatever a boy was used to at home we try to give him here. Once a tough marine even asked me to kiss him good night. He was lonesome for his mother. So I kissed him."[2]

Considering the number of servicemen interacting with one another, it was a feather in Anne's cap that there were no rules — civilian or military; the

Child star Roddy McDowell was the Canteen's youngest volunteer.

boys responded to the easy atmosphere by taking personal responsibility to preserve it. The only requirement for sleeping privileges was the registration of one's name, serial number and outfit.

With so many young men coming and going, with so much music and laughter, talking and pool splashing, Mom's place was not the quietest house on the block. When neighbors complained about the noise, Mrs. Lehr stood up for her boys. "They are going to enjoy themselves. If you don't like it, you can go sit in a foxhole for them!"[3]

Eventually, Anne had 1,000 civilian women volunteers who pitched in with cleaning, washing dishes, sewing, making beds, waiting tables and dancing with servicemen. During the three years of the war, the Guild saw well over a million men sleeping, eating and playing at this welcoming, free hostelry, including fighting men from all the United Nations.

American G.I.s could share songs and stories with British Grenadier Guardsmen and Australian fliers, or play ping-pong with Chinese pilots, Dutch sailors and French Merchant Marines. Here, at Mom's place, the ideal of world harmony was actually happening. After the foreign and American servicemen left the Guild, they sent gifts and letters to Anne Lehr from all over the world. Mail averaged fifty letters a day, which Mrs. Lehr answered faithfully.

As the number of guests increased, so did the Guild's expenses, and as countless mothers have done through the ages, Mom Lehr worried about how she would make ends meet. Average operating costs were approximately $4,000 a week, with most of the budget going for food. The monthly laundry bill was about $1300.

At first, financial assistance came from diverse sources. There were individual donations ranging from a dollar to $200, with more substantial checks sent from time to time by such industry people as actors Lew Ayres and Monty Woolley. N.T.G. took nightly collections at his Florentine Gardens nightclub, which amounted to around $1,000 a week; Earl Carroll's organization ("Through These Portals Pass the Most Beautiful Girls in the World"), headed by Beryl Wallace, came up with an average of $3,000 a month. Though all of this assistance was welcomed,

Columnist Hedda Hopper and actress Ann Sheridan oblige the autograph hounds.

it was piecemeal. Even with the proceeds from an occasional movie premiere or prizefight, there simply were not enough funds, and soon the Guild was on the ropes with $25,000 in debt.

It was W.R. Wilkerson who saved the day. Bill Wilkerson, owner of *The Hollywood Reporter*, wrote an editorial in his influential trade paper praising Anne Lehr's valuable contributions to the war. He appealed to the movie studios to give the Guild financial support on a regular basis. Columnists Louella Parsons and Hedda Hopper, along with other established members of the entertainment community, echoed his plea and the movie industry went into action.

Jules Stein — head of Music Corporation of America and the man who helped Bette Davis launch the Hollywood Canteen — was part of a three-man committee that handled the Guild's finances (which lifted the burden of money management from Mrs. Lehr's shoulders). The major studios collectively gave $40,000 a year and the many smaller ones, $50,000. The Hollywood Canteen, while not connected to the Hollywood Guild and Canteen, was in great solidarity with what it was accomplishing and contributed $52,000 annually. Bette and the board liked knowing that when a serviceman who did not have to return to a base or a ship left the Canteen he would find a safe haven at Mom's place.

In theory, the Guild was governed by a Board of Directors, among which were Bette Davis, Myrna Loy, Mary Pickford, Janet Gaynor, Mervyn LeRoy, Mary (Mrs. John) Ford and Jules Stein; in practice, all direction came from Anne Lehr alone. She was tireless — arriving at work at 6:00 PM and staying until early the next morning. And if running the Guild wasn't demanding enough, Lehr opened her own residence to ten young civilian women who needed lodging.

Anne Lehr did not stop helping servicemen after the war ended. She worked with rehabilitation programs and maintained a job-finding bureau for discharged men. Many ex-soldiers still called the Guild home while going to schools on the G.I. Bill of Rights.

The Hollywood Guild and Canteen finally closed within a couple of years of the end of the war. Until her death in November, 1951, Anne Lehr continued to receive letters from the grateful men who would never forget her.

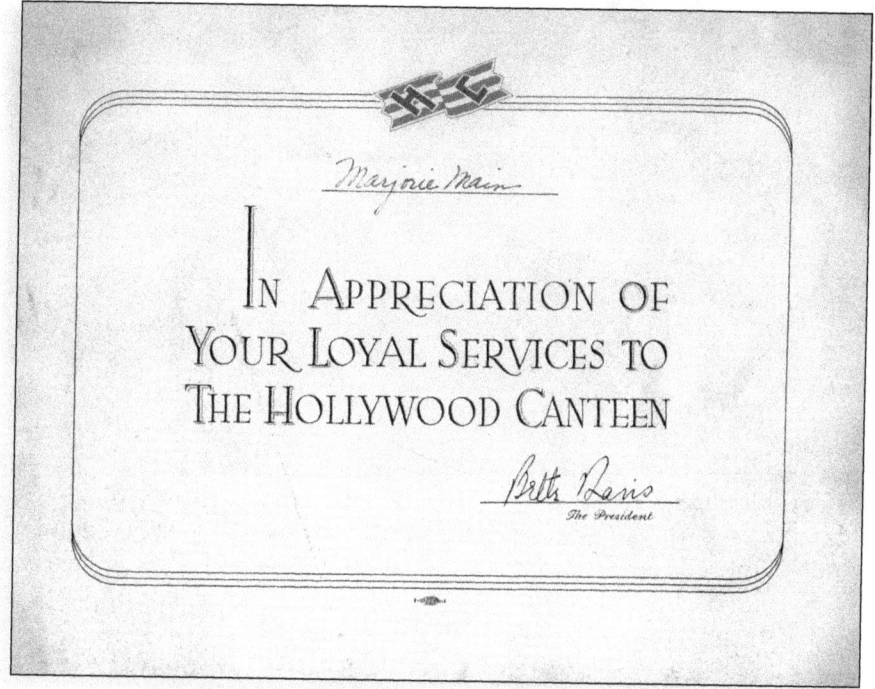

Certificate of Appreciation from Bette Davis to Marjorie Main.

Faye Emerson happily signs autographs for the boys.

As he arrives to volunteer, Red Skelton is stopped by autograph-seeking fans.

CHAPTER 14
CANTEEN ON THE SCREEN

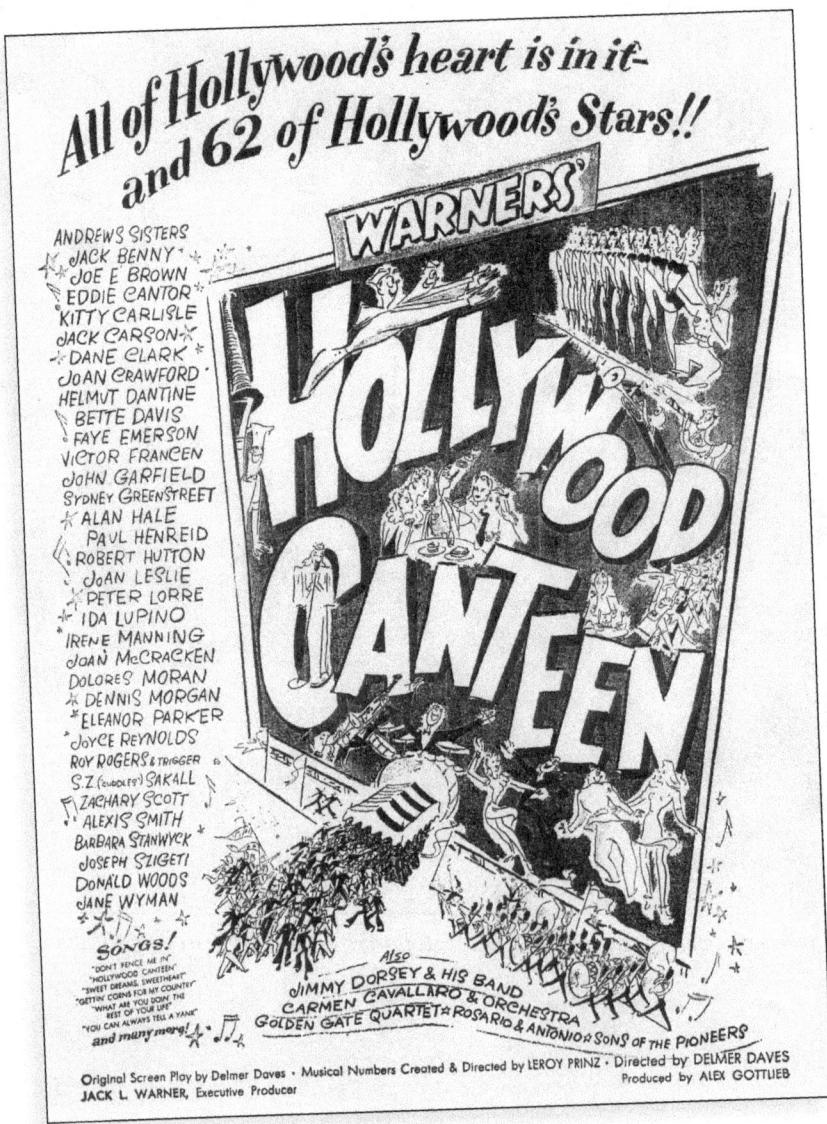

Poster for the Warner Bros. film, Hollywood Canteen *(1944).*

Warner Bros.' *Hollywood Canteen* (1944), was part of a group of movies unique to the war years during the studio system: the all-star, patriotic musical comedy. These staples presented famous players of a particular studio performing within light storylines created to showcase their talents. Though *Hollywood Canteen* would become the most popular of these celebrity-rich cavalcades, it was not among the first.

Paramount's *Star-Spangled Rhythm* (1942), starring Betty Hutton, was filled with cameos from Bob Hope and Bing Crosby to Cecil B. DeMille. United Artists' *Stage Door Canteen* (1943) offered a roster of theatrical personalities such as Helen Hayes, Alfred Lunt and Lynn Fontanne, and boasted the only screen appearance of the legendary actress Katharine Cornell. *Thank Your Lucky Stars* (1943), from Warner Bros., is best remembered for Bette Davis singing "They're Either Too Young Or Too Old," and dancing a vigorous jitterbug. Other studios' efforts included MGM's Technicolor extravaganza *Thousands Cheer* (1943), and Universal Pictures' *Follow The Boys* (1944), in which Orson Welles did a magic act with Marlene Dietrich.

As the real Stage Door Canteen was the antecedent of the Hollywood Canteen, so it was with the films. Not long after the New York servicemen's center opened in March of 1942, Hollywood producer Sol Lesser (*Our Town*, 1940) began production on a picture about it. *Stage Door Canteen*'s original screenplay was by Delmer Daves, a writer

Movie fans surround a group of celebrities, including Robert Hutton, who are attending the premiere of the Warner Bros. film, Hollywood Canteen.

(Love Affair, 1939) who would later become a successful director *(Destination Tokyo*, 1943; *3:10 To Yuma*, 1957). When Jules Stein learned that *Stage Door* was in the works, he persuaded Sol Lesser to contribute 25% of the film's profits to the Hollywood Canteen.

Stein then convinced Warner Bros. to make a movie about the Hollywood Canteen, with a screenplay written by Delmer Daves. How could Warners say no to a subject that was right in its own back yard? Not only did the studio green light the project, it offered to pay an advance of $250,000 to the Hollywood Canteen (officially for the rights to the name and the concept), along with 40% of the profits, less 25% of production costs. And, through the efforts of Sol Lesser, Warner Bros. and the Hollywood Canteen agreed to donate 25% of the $250,000 advance to the Stage Door Canteen.

The idea was to have the stars play themselves on screen, interacting with servicemen as they really did at the Hollywood Canteen, and have the G.I.s portrayed by actors and extras. Delmer Daves, who would also be the film's director, wrote bits into his screenplay for the stars assuming that they would be paid on a prorated salary basis, according to the length of each role. Under producer Jesse Lasky (*Sergeant York*, 1941), Daves started shooting on November 21, 1943.

But *Hollywood Canteen* was only before the cameras until December 11, when the production was shut down due to a major dispute with the Screen Actors Guild. From Warner Bros.' viewpoint,

Actor Robert Hutton shakes Bette Davis' hand during the filming of the Warner Bros. movie, Hollywood Canteen. *The movie set, built at the studio, closely resembled the real Hollywood Canteen.*

prorating actors' salaries to make such a star-studded picture seemed the only way to afford it — especially when the studio was donating a lot of money to the Canteen. However, S.A.G had a rule # 33, which prohibited salary cuts or prorates for its actors in commercial films. If the rule were upheld, Warners would have had to pay a star as much as $150,000 for an hour's work. And the union was not only against reductions in salaries of Warners' contract players, it did not want the studio to exert pressure — such as pushing "patriotism" — on free lance actors to accept cuts either.

The *Canteen* sound stages remained dark for nearly six months while Warner Bros. and S.A.G. crossed legal swords. In support of its members, S.A.G. maintained that non-contract players must receive full salary, regardless of the brevity of their appearances. Warners countered by filing a damage suit for $500,000 against the guild, claiming that that was the amount which the studio had already spent on pre-production costs and on filming before the shut-down.

The case never got to court. An amicable arrangement was reached when the guild relaxed its edict against prorating the salaries of both contract players and free-lance artists, and Warner Bros., in turn, consented not to ask other studios for the loan of their stars on a prorated basis.

A single day — a single scene — in the making of a movie can have a tremendous impact on the whole. So does nearly six months of not making

Left to right: Sydney Greenstreet, Robert Hutton and Dane Clark, three stars of the movie, Hollywood Canteen, *serve food and milk at the real Canteen's snack bar, while Una O'Connor lends a hand.*

a movie. *Hollywood Canteen* went back into business with rehearsals starting on May 15, 1944, and filming resumed on June 6th. But as time passes in Hollywood, changes in production, script and cast were inevitable. Alex Gottlieb (*Pardon My Sarong*, 1942) replaced Jesse Lasky as producer. Ann Sheridan, who was to have been the female lead,

Sheet music for the most popular song from the movie, Hollywood Canteen.

had to go on to do *The Doughgirls* (1944), and Joan Leslie took over as the picture's star. Having had its schedule interrupted for almost half a year made *Hollywood Canteen* the last of the all-star war musicals to be released. (Coming to theatres after similar films had already been seen could have reduced its impact had its very title and impressive cast not made it such a draw.)

Three other stars, Robert Hutton, Dane Clark, and Janis Paige, joined Joan Leslie in carrying out the picture's little story through which the Canteen's entertainment could be shown.

Slim Green (Hutton) is a shy soldier from the pacific theatre on leave in Hollywood with his buddy, Sergeant Nolan, aka "Brooklyn" (Clark). Slim wants nothing more than to meet his favorite movie star, Joan Leslie. "She looks like the kind of girl you can walk right up to and say hello." When Slim visits the Hollywood Canteen and Bette Davis, Jane Wyman and John Garfield learn of this sweet kid's longing for Leslie, they decide to help him out — especially Garfield — who arranges an introduction in which Joan gives Slim a kiss.

After Nolan hears about Slim's good time at the Canteen and great fortune of meeting Leslie, he accompanies his pal back to the Canteen the next night. *He* gets to dance with Joan Crawford, but really connects with Angela (Paige), a cute Canteen hostess definitely more his type. The following day, while sightseeing at the Farmer's Market, who should the boys run into but Joan Leslie? If that isn't enough, as Slim enters the Canteen later in the evening, he turns out to be the Millionth Man.[1] Accompanying the honor are all kinds of perks, the best of which is a date with the actress of his choice — Joan, of course. After they go out, Slim and Joan sit together in her back yard, talking, getting closer. The next night, Slim has dinner with Joan and her family (Joan's sister is played by her real-life sister, Betty Brodel).

Slim finds that Joan is as warm and down-to-earth as he knew she would be; Joan recognizes an endearing goodness in Slim (as acted by Hutton, he has a Jimmy Stewart-like quality). "You're nice, Slim. I like being with you." The movie star and the shy soldier are falling in love.

On his last night at the Canteen, Slim gives a pep talk to the assembled servicemen to make up for not having said what was on his heart when he became the Millionth Man. "All I said [then] was 'Golly.'" Joan has promised to take Slim to the railroad station as he heads back to war, but runs out of gas on the way to pick him up. He gets another ride and she arrives at the platform as his train is about to pull out. A helpful G.I. gives Joan a boost up to Slim's open window and the sweethearts kiss goodbye. The movie ends with a close-up of Bette

Davis addressing the troops: "Wherever you go," she says, looking straight into the camera, " our hearts go with you."

With the plot bringing Slim to the Canteen every night of his furlough, there were plenty of opportunities for Warners to parade its stars, as well as those from other studios. Some of the cast included the Andrews Sisters, Jack Benny, Joe E. Brown, Eddie Cantor, Kitty Carlisle, Jack Carson, Joan Crawford, Helmut Dantine, Bette Davis, Faye Emerson, Victor Francen, John Garfield, Mary Gordon, Sydney Greenstreet, Alan Hale, Paul Henreid, Peter Lorre, Ida Lupino, Irene Manning, Joan McCracken, Dolores Moran, Dennis Morgan, Eleanor Parker, Roy Rogers and Trigger, S. Z. Sakall, Alexis Smith, Zachary Scott, Barbara Stanwyk, Craig Stevens and Jane Wyman. Bette Davis, who made *Canteen* while shooting *Mr. Skeffington* (1944), joined by John Garfield, present a history of the Hollywood Canteen supported by documentary-style footage.

Musical offerings came from such headliners as Jimmy Dorsey and his Band, Carmen Cavallero and his Orchestra, and the Sons of the Pioneers. Highlights were "Tumbling Tumbleweeds," performed by the Pioneers, "What Are You Doing The Rest Of Your Life?" sung by Jane Wyman and Jack Carson, and "The Bee," a violin solo played by Joseph Szigeti, followed by "Souvenir," a humorous duet with Szigeti and Jack Benny. Three songs from the movie would become immediate hits: "Sweet Dreams, Sweetheart," sung by Kitty Carlisle, the

Hedy Lamarr and Irene Dunne serve up more autographs.

Andrews Sisters' rendition of "Getting Corns For My Country," and Cole Porter's beautiful "Don't Fence Me In," introduced by Roy Rogers. The studio also used their newly developed, technically improved, recording equipment for the first time in *Canteen*.

LeRoy Prinz created and directed the movie's many song and dance numbers. Prinz, whose first picture was in 1929 and who showed versatility as a dance director in films ranging from *Yankee Doodle Dandy* (1943) to *The Ten Commandments* (1956), put in 61 days of rehearsing routines, which took 28 days to shoot.

Though various publicity blurbs maintained that Warners built a set that was an "exact replica" of the genuine Canteen, there were some minor differences between the real thing and its counterpart on the studio's Sound Stage Four. Nevertheless, the casual-looking wooden structures in which the on-set crowds interacted would make audiences think that they were seeing the world-famous club itself. A sense of reality was added by some location photography, from shots of the Hollywoodland sign to scenes on the Warner Bros. lot.

Hollywood Canteen finished shooting on August 31, 1944. Its ad campaign hailed it as the movie with "All of Hollywood's heart in it and 62 of Hollywood's stars." The picture had its west coast premiere on December 20th at the Warner Theatre on Hollywood Boulevard, just three blocks from the actual Hollywood Canteen. As with the *The Talk of the Town* fundraising premiere/party that kicked off the Canteen in 1942, there were no kliegs and searchlights in front of the theatre because of the war. But by the end of 1944, Hollywood fans

U.S. Vice President Henry Wallace, Dinah Shore and Bob Hope share a good laugh washing dishes.

had grown used to dimmed down openings and big crowds gathered to watch *Canteen*'s premiere activities and the celebrities who turned out for the star-packed film.

When prints of *Hollywood Canteen* were shipped to soldiers serving overseas, they gave the boys who had never been to the Hollywood club a taste of what it was like. And as the film reached screens all over America in 1945, it let civilians in on the kind of entertainment that had only been available to servicemen in Hollywood. In those days before television, people sitting in darkened movie theatres could finally put faces to the musical sounds that they had heard on phonograph records and the radio. Now a Canteen soldier's mom in Milford, Iowa, might get a sense of what her son had written home about.

While the general public responded well to *Hollywood Canteen*, professional reviews were mixed. The main fault found by negative critics was that the film came across as being too self-congratulatory. Kate Cameron in the *New York Daily News* complained of "its complete lack of reserve in singing the praises of Hollywood." [2]

On the other hand, *Variety* wrote: "There isn't a marquee big enough to hold all the names in this one, so how can it miss? Besides, it's basically solid. It has story, cohesion, and heart. That's not a bad parlay, either." [3] Thirty years after *Canteen*'s release, film historians Rudy Behlmer and Tony Thomas pointed out the importance of the picture's "rare moments," citing Joseph Szigeti's and Jack Benny's violin duet and Roy Rogers' singing of "Don't Fence Me In." [4]

Hollywood Canteen received three Academy Award nominations in the categories of Best Sound, Best Scoring, and Best Song — "Sweet Dreams, Sweetheart" (which lost to "Swinging On A Star" from *Going My Way*, 1944).

The passage of time has been on *Hollywood Canteen*'s side. Much of what once may have seemed too sentimental or overblown may be enjoyed in retrospect as an expression of an earnest, far more innocent period in America and in American filmmaking. Joan Leslie's special role — playing her movie-star self, a faithful Canteen volunteer, and the focus of a romance, however contrived — has given the picture a certain lasting charm as Leslie remains one of the most beloved actresses of Hollywood's Golden Age.

And, over the decades, with *Hollywood Canteen*'s availability on television, video and DVD, this "fairly pleasing entertainment…serves as a reminder that once there was such a canteen in Hollywood and that it did provide admirable services for the services." [5]

Two MPs receive a smile and coffee from Rudy Vallee.

Wearing her "HC" armband, Marjorie Reynolds signs another autograph book.

Buster Keaton pours punch for thirsty servicemen at the snack bar.

CANTEEN ON THE SCREEN

From the second-floor window, at the left of the stage, officers and their guests were able to view the Canteen's nightly activities.

Bunny Waters helps Al Ybarra hang photos of actors, who are in the Armed Services, on the Canteen's Hall of Honor wall.

John Garfield visits with Judy Garland during the Canteen's First Birthday party.

With hundreds of soldiers looking on, Ginger Rogers cuts a cake for the guys whose birthdays are being celebrated that night.

After participating in a floor show, regular volunteer Rita Hayworth cuts pies in the kitchen.

CHAPTER 15
"WE'LL MEET AGAIN…" CLOSING THE CANTEEN

When victory over Japan (V-J Day) was announced, nearly everyone in Hollywood took to the streets. While a celebrant displays the Los Angeles Times, *a newsboy is selling out his supply of papers.*

Part of the Canteen's thriving atmosphere was due to a certain split personality. On one hand, the club was a haven from the war. It was at the Canteen that soldiers could suspend their anxieties about what might lie ahead for them, or where they could forget, for just a few hours, what they had already been through. On the other hand, news of how the war was going was an inevitable topic of conversation all over the country, and that included the Canteen. "The sadness of war was all around us," hostess Yvonne De Carlo wrote, "but so was the electrical charge of the common cause."[1]

While hostesses danced with G.I.s to such songs as "I Had The Craziest Dream Last Night" and "Moonlight Becomes You," 1943 saw the Japanese pulling back from Guadalcanal, Italy falling to the Allies, and Germany being walloped by Russia. The prices paid for these and each phase of every victory were inestimable; some were visible at the Hollywood Canteen. Hostesses found increasing use for "Hints on how to treat wounded vets" which Bette Davis had given them. "Forget the wounds, remember the man," the mimeographed instructions said. "Don't be over-solicitous, nor too controlled to the point of indifference. Learn to use the word, 'prosthetics' instead of 'artificial limbs.' Never say, 'it could have been worse.' And when he talks of his war experiences, *listen*, but don't ask for more details than he wants to give."[2]

Hostesses told each other about their encounters with the disabled veterans. Some of their stories were recorded by Kay Proctor, who wrote about a 21 year-old Marine blinded at Guadalcanal. Brought to the Canteen by two Navy nurses, he sat silent and

Thousands of Hollywood residents spent most of V-J day, and night, near the corner of Hollywood and Vine. Traffic lights were disregarded and traffic was brought to a standstill.

motionless until the floor show began. After Betty Hutton sang "the nonsensical words to 'Murder, He Says' and Eddie Cantor cracked joke after joke," the young man began to chuckle. Soon "he was rocking with…full-bellied laughter. One of the nurses said to Bette Davis, " 'I thank God for this place! That's the first laugh from that boy's lips since we left Guadalcanal!'"

Another night Proctor met a soldier who "had lost both legs in a South Seas battle which had cost his twin brother's life." Though he had learned to walk well on his prosthetics, "he hadn't had the nerve" to try dancing till Kay encouraged him. After leading him "out in the middle where its so crowded no one will notice us anyway…he managed exceptionally well and no one would have guessed his difficulty. When the dance ended," Kay wrote, "I introduced him to Deanna Durbin and off they whirled when the next dance began. He sought me out later, all smiles and confidence. 'Gosh,' he said, 'if I can dance with Deanna Durbin, I can dance with the world!'" [3]

By 1944, twelve million Americans were in uniform. On some nights, it must have seemed to Bette Davis that every one of them had been through the Hollywood Canteen. Davis could look across the floor at her fellow performers as they served coffee to sailors, danced with boys from the Coast Guard and the Air Force, schmoozed with Marines, and knew first hand how hard it was for them to work at a studio all day and be vivacious at night. ("Thank God," she would say, "I was blessed with so much energy!") [4] Davis had made many a frantic phone call to this actor or that actress to fill in at the last minute for someone who couldn't show up. She deeply appreciated everyone who helped, even — maybe especially — Jack Warner, as she was "on the phone all day long" between takes on her films and "he never beefed." [5] (While they were entertaining soldiers who were off to fight the war in Asia, many Canteen stars were "fighting" it on soundstages in Burbank, Hollywood and Culver City, making morale-boosting war movies — often in the same ones — such as John Garfield and Faye Emerson in *Air Force*, 1943; Garfield, Emerson and Alan Hale in *Destination Tokyo*, 1943; Marsha Hunt and Ann Southern in *Cry Havoc*, 1943; Irene Dunne and Spencer Tracy in *A Guy Named Joe*, 1943.)

As 1944 — with such tide-turning victories as the Allies' invasion of Normandy on June 6th — became1945, there was cautious optimism in the air. Words of progress notwithstanding, members of the Armed Forces needed the Canteen's hospitality as much as ever, even as differences in the men were apparent. "As the war went on year after year," Davis wrote, "one could not help notice the change in the age of the G.I. s. They were all much younger and less robust. British servicemen looking not more than sixteen years old who were on their way to the South Pacific came to the Canteen." [6]

Though the United States entered World War II fighting on two fronts at the same time, the conflicts could not end simultaneously. The Allies' success in Europe culminated in the spring of 1945 when Italian partisans executed Benito Mussolini on April 28th, and Adolph Hitler committed suicide on April 30th. In May, Italy and Germany surrendered and V-E Day (Victory in Europe) on May 8th was celebrated throughout most of the world.

As Hollywood served G.I.s heading for the South Pacific, the Canteen remained as crowded as ever, and V-E Day found every host and hostess, serviceman and woman exuberant over the defeat of the Nazis. Then, after the Americans dropped devastating

An entry in a hostess' autograph book.

atomic bombs on Hiroshima on August 6th and on Nagasaki on August 9th, Japan, too, agreed to an unconditional surrender on August 14th.

President Truman proclaimed September 2nd — when Japan and the Allies signed the official surrender agreement — as V-J Day (Victory over Japan). The announcement brought a profound collective sigh of relief that after three years, eight months and 22 days since Japan's sneak attack on Pearl Harbor, the Second World War was finally over.

Along with the rest of the nation, people in Hollywood were euphoric at the news of peace. Movie studios, offices, businesses and shops closed; traffic came to a complete standstill. Cheering crowds jammed the intersection of Hollywood and Vine to a cacophony of shouts, sirens, horns and whistles that continued till the wee small hours of the morning.

Probably nowhere in town was the elation higher than it was at 1451 North Cahuenga Boulevard. Three blocks from Hollywood and Vine, the Hollywood Canteen was a magnet gathering spot for film industry celebrants who whooped it up with the servicemen for whom war's end meant the most.

Marlene Dietrich, returning from a European tour, was thrilled to be a hostess on that night and kissed as many men in uniform as she could. Bette Davis, who was the evening's Master of Ceremonies, performed several skits with other stars and a number of eager young soldiers. On this "anything goes" occasion, she even participated in a pie-throwing act. At the microphone where she had stood so many times before, Bette heard her voice catch more than once as she spoke to a jubilant, packed house.

The end of the war, which was causing changes all over the world, led to the difficult decision to close the Hollywood Canteen. The question was when. Though soldiers were still visiting the famous nightspot, there were fewer of them coming every

Servicemen packed the dance floor every night.

week. After a meeting of the Board of Directors, it was announced on August 30th that the Canteen would shut its doors after celebrating its third anniversary on October 3rd.

The news was not well received by visiting servicemen and there were still enough of them to give the Board pause. Appeals from the boys, the volunteer workers and musical organizations, made Bette Davis send out telegrams calling for a special meeting of the Board on Tuesday evening, September 11th at the Canteen's publicity office, 6506 Sunset Blvd. "Because of the great number of petitions received against closing the Canteen October 3rd…" a new date had to be set. [7]

The Board agreed to keep the Canteen open until Thanksgiving Day. This was not long enough for the Ernie Pyle Post No. 626 of the American Legion, which passed a resolution opposing the November cutoff, and recommended keeping the Canteen open through New Year's Eve. Board members were sympathetic to the request. They knew that there were still soldiers far from home in need of entertainment. They understood that the Canteen's job was not finished and saw shutting it down on Thanksgiving as a regrettable necessity. However, they had an expanded vision.

Two months before the Canteen would go dark, the Board had formed the Hollywood Canteen Foundation, designed to administer the remaining funds in the Canteen's bank account. Of the $500,000 that would be transferred to the Foundation when the Canteen closed, $390,000 had

Jane Powell signs hundreds of autographs after performing on stage.

come from Warner Bros.' payments to the Canteen for its share from the profits of *Stage Door Canteen* and *Hollywood Canteen*; the rest was from donations.

As Virginia Wright, Drama Editor of *The Daily News* would put it, "Rather than deplete the Canteen's resources by keeping the hall open for servicemen passing through town it is the board's carefully considered opinion that money can be used to greater advantage for veterans in fields of education, rehabilitation or hospitals." [8]

On November 22, the line of servicemen stretched along Sunset Boulevard, turned the corner at Cahuenga and headed south as each G.I. prepared to enter the Canteen for the last time.

The festivities began at 2:00 in the afternoon and, everyone was happy to learn, would extend beyond the usual midnight closing time. The nonstop entertainment was supplied by many of the soldiers' favorite artists — both at home and overseas: Bob Hope, Jerry Colonna, Jack Benny, Dinah Shore, Hedy Lamarr, Jack Carson, James Stewart, Henry Fonda, Ingrid Bergman, Joan Leslie, Janis Paige, Edward G. Robinson, Ronald Colman, and, of course, Bette Davis. A number of others, such as Roddy McDowall, James Gleason, Billie Burke, Bonita Granville and Jack Haley also appeared.

Hope and Benny made the bittersweet event buoyant as they kept the laughs coming. On a serious note, Hope — who had done a number of his radio shows from that same tiny stage — said that leaving the Canteen would be "like leaving old friends. I have always thrilled in the thought of entertaining our [military] men and women." [9]

Junior hostesses would not remember how many sailors they danced with or how many soldiers sang along with the comforting song…"We'll meet again, don't know where, don't know when, but I know we'll meet again some sunny day…" A powerful moment was when Kay Kyser, whose band had played at the Canteen's opening and on almost every Saturday night thereafter, bid a tearful goodbye to a grateful audience, then led his musicians in "The Star-Spangled Banner."

Long-faithful hostesses realized that they would be missing the Canteen as much as the young men they served. One such senior hostess, Lucille La Plant, had corresponded with approximately 1000 servicemen a month since the Canteen began. "Sure, the boys came here looking for glamour," the *Herald Examiner* reported a volunteer as saying, "but they surprised even themselves when they found as much if not more pleasure in the motherliness and guidance of our senior hostesses." [10]

The *Examiner* went on to point out that junior hostesses who had danced "an estimated 1,640,250 miles with the boys [and] the actors and actresses who worked in the kitchen and snack bar…had found an outlet for serving America's heroes and had made many friends — some who would never return — at… the country's premiere servicemen's center." [11]

If there was anyone who could diffuse whatever sadness was in the room, it was the indomitable Bette Davis. As she described the goals of the Hollywood Canteen Foundation, with its $500,00 in an irrevocable trust to be administered for the benefit of veterans, she helped the crowd see that something beautiful was not so much ending as being transformed.

The Canteen would close "in a blaze of glory. Everyone kissed everyone. Tears were as conspicuous as G.I. s." In recognition of her service, Bette was presented with "a gold pin, a facsimile of the Canteen crest, with her initials set in diamonds and rubies." [12] She, in turn, expressed her gratitude for the umpteenth time to all the volunteers for their unstinting support. She would always admire particularly the ones who "outlived the first flush of publicity and novelty" and continued working at the Canteen for the duration. [13] Throughout the long day and evening, she had several opportunities to bid emotional farewells to the servicemen who had always "made me so proud." [14] After more than twelve hours of dancing, singing, eating, drinking and being entertained, the last soldier walked out the doors that had welcomed three million servicemen for over three years. Thanksgiving was, after all, the right time for closing the Hollywood Canteen. There was so much to be thankful for.

EPILOGUE

As the war solved immense problems and created new ones and maps overseas and mores everywhere were altered forever, Hollywood reflected the nation's inevitable shifts. Hard looks were taken at the plight of returning veterans in such films as Edward Dmytryk's *Till The End Of Time* (1946) and William Wyler's *The Best Years Of Our Lives* (1946). And if the movie industry had been reshaped by war and its aftermath, so was the town — not the least by the Hollywood Canteen.

According to *People* magazine, "…what changed Hollywood was the [C]anteen during World War II. All through the war there were about a million servicemen in the area, and every one of them had to come and see Hollywood. So a tremendous number of opportunistic owners put in retail operations to service the G.I.s…"[1]

The welcome that soldiers found at the Canteen left a good taste in their mouths for Hollywood. When former hostess, Diane Meredith, considered the effects the Canteen had on the young men, she said, "Even after the war, it made some difference in their views of the world, to [have been] so close to so many creative people…was marvelous."[2]

Certainly many servicemen who had visited the Canteen were later drawn back to the vicinity as civilians to buy homes and attend schools on the G.I. Bill. With their uniforms packed away, they settled in Southern California along with the men and women who had come from all over the country to work in the defense industry and stayed on. The population of Hollywood and its environs grew, became more ethnically diverse and pulsed with post-war possibilities.

The Hollywoodland sign in the hills that the boys remembered from their Canteen days would soon have its last four letters omitted, eventually becoming the most iconic town symbol in the world.

Not long after the Hollywood Canteen closed, a group of investors headed by Thomas Lee and Guy Francis formed a business called Creative Enterprises, Inc. and leased the former Canteen building. There, like a hermit crab, it tried to move in to the renowned site with a nightclub using the name, "Hollywood Canteen." When Bette Davis got wind of this, she announced the filing of a lawsuit by the true Hollywood Canteen, which sought an injunction to stop Creative Enterprises from using the famous name.

The complaint stated that the defendants erected a sign on the front of the building which said "Hollywood Canteen" in large letters — with the word "former" in very small print. The Hollywood Canteen must have prevailed; the misleading nightclub apparently didn't open anywhere, as the name never appeared in any telephone directories or subsequent newspaper articles.

Over the next several years, the Hollywood Canteen building housed such venues as the Golden Spike Theater and the Le Grand Comedy Theater — the latter occupying the premises until 1965. Then, on December 20, 1966, a wrecking crew arrived and reduced the landmark at 1451 North Cahuenga Boulevard to dust. As a bulldozer ploughed through rotting walls and wooden beams, one of the few people to witness the demolition was Janis Paige, whose career had begun at the Hollywood Canteen. The only items that were salvaged were an electric exit sign and three forecourt slabs of cement in which some soldiers had written their names and put their handprints. These mementos were given to Janis, who displayed them at her home in Los Angeles.[3]

The outbreak of the Korean conflict in June of 1950 called the Hollywood Canteen into action again. Its new Board of Directors included President Bette Davis, Jules Stein, John te Groen, Delmer Daves, Mary Ford, Mervyn LeRoy, Sol Lesser, Chef Milani, Mack Millar, Baron Morehead, Mason Morris, Cameron Shipp and Al Ybarra. At the direction of Jules Stein, the Hollywood Canteen Foundation bought the former Florentine Gardens nightclub at 5955 Hollywood Blvd. to provide the Canteen with a permanent home where members of the Armed Forces and movie stars could meet during national emergencies. After being purchased in November, 1950, the building underwent extensive remodeling to prepare it for the expected servicemen.

The new Canteen opened on July 4, 1951. It varied from the original in ways beyond the obvious of not being in a homey, rustic atmosphere. Times had changed in the six years since the end of WW II. This was a different war and the amount of servicemen traveling through Hollywood was far from what it had been in the early 1940s. (Also, the Canteen was no longer the only servicemen's club in the neighborhood. The USO had opened its center at 1710 North Ivar Avenue on February 17, 1951.)

Unlike the first Hollywood Canteen, where entertainment and dancing were nightly attractions, this one operated only on Saturday and Sunday evenings, when it offered free sandwiches, coffee, soft drinks and dancing. The Canteen at the old Florentine Gardens functioned until the mid-nineteen fifties, when it was taken over by the Hollywood USO. The club served its purpose admirably, but it will always be the original 1940s haven on Cahuenga, with its top name entertainment and most glamorous stars, that will always mean "the Hollywood Canteen" to the world.

After Turner Classic Movies aired the movie, *Hollywood Canteen* on a television broadcast, July 23, 2008, TCM host, Robert Osborne said about

In 1951, the Hollywood Canteen Foundation purchased the former Florentine Gardens nightclub on Hollywood Boulevard as a facility to serve soldiers during the Korean conflict.

the real Canteen, "Any soldier still around who went there will tell you it's one experience they never, *ever* forgot." Former Marine James Washburn, definitely hasn't forgotten. Sixty-five years later, Washburn, who spent part of the war in a Japanese prison camp, recalls that he endured the pain of the brutal beatings he received at the hands of his captors "by remembering the beautiful music I heard at the Hollywood Canteen."[4]

And servicemen never forgot the girls. Since the end of the war, actresses who had volunteered at the Canteen have had men come up to them across the decades as they've all aged and say, "I danced with you at the Hollywood Canteen!" Bette Davis, who did everything but dance, found that her identity with the Canteen, *as* the Canteen, never stopped. "To this day," she wrote in *This 'n' That*, "I often meet men who tell me they had been to the Hollywood Canteen and what a thrill it was for them to see and talk to the stars…"[5]

On November 6, 1950, Davis put her handprints and footprints in cement at Grauman's Chinese Theatre in connection with her triumphant performance in *All About Eve* (1950). Even this event was enhanced by her association with the Hollywood Canteen. "On the day of her footprint ceremony she was assisted by Canteen Marine Corps veterans Staff Sergeant Jack Spencer and Technical Sergeant Bert R. Nave as a tribute to her work as president of the organization."[6]

Over forty years after the Canteen first opened, Bette Davis was given the Distinguished Civilian Service Medal for "having founded and run the Hollywood Canteen all during World War II."[7] Since co-founder John Garfield's death in 1952, Bette became the main representative of their

Bette Davis attended the 1983 Military Ball, where she was presented with the Distinguished Civilian Service Medal for her founding of the Hollywood Canteen.

venture. And she had always been the tornado, the indefatigable star worker. Or, as a Garfield biographer put it, "It was her clout which turned [John's] idea into a reality."[8] The rarely bestowed medal, representing the highest honor conferred on a civilian, was presented to Davis at the Army's Annual Ball on June 11, 1983 at the Beverly Hilton Hotel.

Servicemen in full dress uniform saluted Davis as she entered the hotel and a military band played a heart-stirring musical welcome. As the theme of this Army Ball was a tribute to the Hollywood Canteen, photographs of Davis and the Canteen covered the foyer's walls. Roy Thorsen, who had instigated Davis' recognition by the Defense Department, produced the after-dinner show, "A Night At The Hollywood Canteen," with Bob Hope as the M.C. Bette's favorite part of the production was watching actors and actresses re-enact an evening at the club which "brought back many memories of the fantastic years at the Canteen."[9]

The medal was awarded to Bette "for meritorious service from 1941 to the present, for contributing to the morale and well-being of millions of servicemen and women." Choosing Davis "...was the unanimous decision of all branches of the armed forces — Army, Navy, Marine and Air Corps."[10]

The citation was wrong on the 1941 date, as the Canteen was founded in 1942, but it was so right in extending the worth of what Davis did "to the present." It was 1983 then, but because of the Hollywood Canteen Foundation, "the present" can and does go on. Bette Davis, who died in 1989, often said, "There are few accomplishments in my life that I am sincerely proud of. The Hollywood Canteen is one of them."[11] She would be even prouder to know that the Hollywood Canteen Foundation, formed shortly before the Canteen closed, is still doing so much good for so many people.

Jules Stein managed the Foundation's treasury, invested it wisely, and ran it up to several million dollars. The Foundation's mission was and is to make charitable contributions to associations that provide services for veterans. It was there for the soldiers coming back from Korea and Vietnam as it was for the G.I.s of WW II. What Dr. Stein, who died in 1981, began so many decades ago, makes it possible for returning veterans of 21st Century wars in Afghanistan and Iraq to receive health care, financial assistance, rehabilitative training and counseling.

In addition to such familiar names as the American Legion, Paralyzed Veterans of America and the USO, other organizations aided by the Hollywood Canteen Foundation include Angel Flight For Veterans, which provides free air transportation to active military and to veterans and their families to distant medical centers; Special Operations Warrior Foundation, which helps children whose parents died in combat to obtain college scholarships; The Jules Stein Eye Institute, which treats veterans' visual problems through collaboration with veterans hospitals.

Focusing on Bette Davis in these pages or paying attention to other stars like Dietrich, Hayworth or Lamarr was inevitable: they truly served and it was their celebrity magnet that helped draw 3,000,000 servicemen to the Canteen. But it was always the unsung ones who kept the wheels turning — "each studio extra, each office clerk, steno and flunky, each member of each Hollywood union...who made the Canteen possible."[12]

Above all, the Hollywood Canteen was the servicemen. Looking at photographs of all the uniforms covering the dance floor, it can seem like "a sea of servicemen." But every single man there had a story, a family, a fear, a dream. These soldiers and sailors who were so young then would become part of what Tom Brokaw has famously called "the greatest generation any society has ever produced."[13] They were "participants in and witness to sacrifices of the highest order...in the greatest war the world has ever seen."[14] Most of them had never been so far from home before and would never forget the comfort they found on Cahuenga Blvd.

With every passing day, there are fewer WWII veterans left to remember the unique club " for servicemen." Here, then, is the record: that once there was a converted barn in the heart of Hollywood that *was* the heart of Hollywood. Once, in the land of the free, the Hollywood Canteen made a home for the brave.

APPENDIX

The photographs in this book give a good idea of the layout of the Hollywood Canteen. But for readers who want more details, the following description offers a thorough sense of what a serviceman saw when he went there.

The building was located on the west side of Cahuenga Blvd. (1451 North Cahuenga Blvd.), just south of the Shell Oil Station on the corner of Sunset Blvd. Shortly after the Canteen opened, a small "One Hour Portrait" photograph store was sandwiched between the Shell station and the Canteen. The front of the Canteen faced east, and had a seven-foot high board fence and gate which insured privacy by keeping out all civilians, except for those actually working there. Outside the fence was the sidewalk, where servicemen lined up to wait their turn to enter the Canteen. After a few months of operation, the Canteen installed a large canopy/awning in the forecourt/patio, between the front of the building and the fence. At the rear of the building, on Cole Place, was both the volunteers' entrance and the stage door entrance. All volunteers, such as hostesses and staff, checked in through the volunteers' entrance. All the celebrities who were scheduled to entertain that day, entered through the stage door.

The Canteen's main entrance, on Cahuenga, which was for the exclusive use of the servicemen, had double doors that opened into a small lobby. This lobby was about eight feet wide and about thirty feet long. On the right side of the lobby was a small check room where men could leave their jackets and caps. To the left of the entrance, at the south end of the lobby, was a telephone booth and stairs that led up to the mezzanine where the stage lights were located. Between the telephone booth and the stairs was a dutch door that led into the offices of the full-time staff of nine people. In the offices, were windows that looked out into the main room. The east wall of the lobby later became the Hall of Honor. On the west wall, which separated the lobby from the main room, was a small bulletin board for servicemen to post messages. Next to the bulletin board was a window that looked into the main room. To the left of the window was the wide entrance opening into the main room. On the left wall of the wide entrance was a list of all the unions and guilds that were sponsors of the Canteen. To the immediate right and left of the entrance were the Military Police (MP) and Shore Patrol (SP) stations, respectively. These two booths offered the members of the MP and SP some of the best seats to watch the evening's entertainment.

In the southeast corner of the main room was an elevated seating area where the "Angels' Tables" were located. It was here that guests, who paid $25 per seat, could watch the servicemen and the entertainment. Along the south wall were the large murals that had been painted by the members of the Motion Picture Illustrators Guild. Placed in front of the wall were tables and chairs where servicemen and hostesses could sit and chat. In the southwest corner was a room that housed all the controls for the stage lights . To the right of this room was an exit which led to the stage door at the rear of the building. Above this exit, and up on the second floor, was a small room with a window that looked out onto the the main room. This room was for the exclusive use of military officers and guests. (Because the Canteen was solely for enlisted men, officers were prohibited from going onto the first floor.) Also upstairs was the fingerprint room where all volunteers were photographed and fingerprinted for their identification cards.

In front of the main room's west wall was an elevated stage on which the many bands played, and celebrities entertained the servicemen. To the right of the stage were the bathrooms and an exit, which led to the volunteers' entrance/exit, at the rear of the building. In the northwest corner of the main room, to the right of the stage, was the kitchen where all the food was prepared and dishes were washed. Also in the rear of the building were storage rooms. Next to the kitchen, on the north wall, was a small seating area with tables and chairs. Along the majority of the north wall was a long service counter, known as the snack bar, where steaming-hot coffee, sandwiches, chilled half-pint cartons of milk, cake, cigarettes, raisins and candy were dispensed by the celebrity volunteers. In front of the counter were tables and chairs for hostesses and servicemen. Above the service counter was the 326 square-foot wall mural, painted by members of the Screen Cartoonists Guild. To the right of the service counter was another exit door and, to the right of that, an additional seating area. In the middle of the main room was a large wooden floor which was used for dancing or standing/sitting to watch the evening's entertainment on stage. Hanging from the main room's gargantuan ceiling beams, were chandeliers made from old wagon wheels. Their pendant kerosene lanterns, which had been converted to electricity, lit up the Canteen for over three years.

APPENDIX

187

The small cloak room in the front lobby was where servicemen checked their caps before entering the main room.

The Canteen's office, which housed the nine salaried employees, was located on the first floor.

APPENDIX

189

The entrance to the main room was on the east wall and displayed a large list of the many unions and guilds that sponsored the Canteen.

The SP (Shore Patrol) station was located on the east wall, next to the main entrance.

Most of the painted murals adorned the south wall of the Canteen.

The Canteen's bandstand was along the west wall.

The snack bar, which was along the north wall, was the hub for food and autographs.

This room on the second story, with a window that looked onto the dance floor and stage, was the only place were officers and their guests could visit the Canteen. Only enlisted men were allowed on the first floor.

The front ot the Canteen, before servicemen line up to enter.

CHAPTER NOTES

Chapter 1
The Heart of the Matter: How It Began
1. Katz, Ephraim. *The Film Encyclopedia (Second Edition)*. Harper Collins, New York, 1994. P. 333

Chapter 2
Hooray For Hollywood
1. Manuscript for an unpublished biography of Jules Stein. Chapter 12, P. 93
2. *San Francisco California People's World Newspaper*, September 8, 1942
3. Ibid.
4. Ibid.
5. Ibid.
6. Ibid.

Chapter 3
Building A Dream
1. Davis, Bette with Michael Herskowitz. *This 'n' That*. G.P. Putnam's Sons. New York. 1987. P. 124

Chapter 5
"All Of Hollywood Is Your Host"
1. *Los Angeles Examiner*, October 4, 1942
2. Ibid

Chapter 6
Day In, Night Out
1. *Hollywood Citizen News*, September 22, 1943
2. Stine, Whitney. *Mother Goddam: The Story Of The Career Of Bette Davis;* With A Running Commentary By Bette Davis. Hawthorn Books. New York, 1974
3. Katz, Ephraim. *The Film Encyclopedia (Second Edition)*. P. 1123
4. *Los Angeles Times*. October 21, 1942. P.14
5. *The Hollywood Reporter*. August 17, 1942
6. Davis, Bette with Michael Herskowitz. *This'n' That*. P.127

Chapter 7
Rules Of The Game
1. A. C. Lyles to authors, August, 2007
2. Porter, Jean. " Donna and Me: Camp Tours of Donna Reed and Jean Porter." *Classic Images*, February, 2006. P. 6
3. Smith, Meg Cole. *Memories of a World War II Bride*
4. Nugent, Frank S. *New York Times Magazine*, October 17, 1943. P. 16

Chapter 8
"What Stars Will Be Here Tonight?"
1. *Screenland Magazine*. November, 1943. P. 84
2. Davis, Bette. *The Lonely Life*: *An Autobiography*. G. P. Putnam's Sons, 1962. P. 261
3. Jean Porter to authors, August 11, 2006
4. Lamarr, Hedy. *Ecstacy and Me: My Life As A Woman*. Bartholomew House, 1966. P. 113
5. Skolsky, Sidney. "Hollywords and Picturegraphs" segment of syndicated column. October 6, 1942
6. Christina Crawford to authors, December 11, 2006
7. Hopper, Hedda. "Screen and Stage," *Los Angeles Times*, July 7, 1943
8. The idea of stars enjoying a bit of ordinary life through their service at the Canteen was suggested by Christina Crawford to authors, December 11, 2006
9. Jean Porter to authors, August 11, 2006

10. Hunt, Marsha. *The Way We Wore: Styles of the 1930s and 1940s and Our World Since Then*. Fallbrook Publishing, Ltd. Fallbrook, California. 1993. P. 298
11. Marsha Hunt to authors, October 4, 2006
12. Marsha Hunt to authors, October 4, 2006

Chapter 9
"Miss Hayworth, May I Have This Dance?"
1. *Milwaukee Journal*. March 7, 1943. P. 96
2. Jane Withers to authors, June, 2006
3. Diane Meredith Volz to authors, July, 2007
4. *Los Angeles Times*. April 19, 1944. P. A1
5. *Los Angeles Times*. May 3, 1944. P. 42
6. *Los Angeles Times*. May 2, 1944
7. Untitled newspaper article. March 29, 1946. authors' collection
8. Joan Leslie to authors, July 27, 2007
9. "Hollywood Canteen" article by Ace Collins. Hollywood Studio Magazine. Nov. 1983. P 7
10. Joan Leslie to authors, July 27, 2007
11. "Hollywood Canteen" article. P. 7
12. Lamarr, Hedy. *Ecstacy and Me: My Life as a Woman*. Bartholomew House. 1966. Pp 113-114
13. Riva, Maria. *Marlene Dietrich by Her Daughter Maria Riva*. Alfred A. Knopf. New York. 1993. P. 525
14. Ibid. P. 526
15. Wood, Ean. *Dietrich: A Biography*. Sanctuary Publishing, Ltd. London, 2002. P. 218
16. Harry Carey, Jr. to authors, May, 2007
17. Howard Johnson to authors, December 4, 2006
18. Kobal, John. *Rita Hayworth: The Time, The Place, The Woman*. W.H. Allen. London. 1977. P. 138
19. Howard Johnson to authors, December 4, 2006

Chapter 10
A Good Time For All: An Integrated Canteen
1. Starr, Kevin. *Embattled Dreams: California in War and Peace 1940-1950*. Oxford University Press. 2002 P. 168
2. Davis, Bette with Michael Herskowitz. *This 'n' That*. G.P. Putnam's Sons. NY, 1987. P. 128
3. Ibid.
4. *Los Angeles Times*. September 3. 1943
5. Diane Meredith Volz to authors, July, 2007
6. James Washburn to authors, October 30, 2007
7. McBride, Joseph. *Searching For John Ford: A Life*. St. Martin's Press. NY 2001. P. 368
8. *Los Angeles Times*. September 3, 1943
9. *Hollywood Canteen News*. December 25, 1942

Chapter 11
The Greatest Show In Town
1. A. C. Lyles to authors, August, 2007
2. *Photoplay*. October, 1943. P. 87
3. Jean Porter to authors, August 11, 2006
4. Stine, Whitney. *Mother Goddam: The Story of the Career of Bette Davis;* With a Running Commentary by Bette Davis. Hawthorn Books. New York, 1974. P. 192
5. Bob Hope radio script, October 13, 1942, courtesy Bob Hope Enterprises

Chapter 12
Special Attractions
1. Invitation to Barn Dance, August, 1945. Hollywood Canteen Files. Margaret Herrick Library, Academy of Motion Picture Arts and Sciences. Beverly Hills, California
2. *Herald Examiner*. November 1, 1943
3. *Los Angeles Times*. November 1, 1943
4. Davis, Bette with Michael Herskowitz. *This 'n' That*. P. 127
5. McGee, Tom. *The Girl With the Million Dollar Legs*. Vestal Press. Vestal, New York. 1995. P. 95
6. Lamarr, Hedy. *Ecstsacy and Me*. P. 114
7. Skolsky, Sidney. Syndicated column, *Hollywood Citizen News*. October 16, 1943
8. Katz, Ephraim. *The Film Encyclopedia* (Second Edition) HarperCollins. New York. 1994. P. 134
9. Tierney, Gene with Mickey Herkowitz. *Self-Portrait*. Wyden Books. 1979/Berkeley Books 1980. New York. Berkeley Edition. Pp 98-99; P.104
10. Ibid. P. 108

Chapter 13
A Place To Stay: The Hollywood Guild And Canteen
1. Boesen, Victor and John Reddy. "G.I. Mom," *Liberty* magazine, June 9, 1945. P. 34
2. Ibid.
3. Ibid.

Chapter 14
Canteen On The Screen
1. The Canteen's real Millionth Man, Sergeant Carl Bell, received $200 from Warner Bros. to incorporate scenes in the film that were similar to his experience. A Hollywood publicist, Mac Millar, who claimed that honoring a millionth man was his sole idea, was paid $15,000. — Warner Bros. Collection, University of Southern California, Los Angeles, California
2. Quirk, Lawrence J. *The Films of Joan Crawford.* The Citadel Press. Seacaucus, New York. 1968. P. 155
3. Ibid.
4. Behlmer, Rudy and Tony Thomas. *Hollywood's Hollywood: The Movies About the Movies.* Citadel Press. Seacaucus, N.J. 1975. P. 296
5. Ibid. P. 297

Chapter 15
"We'll Meet Again..." Closing The Canteen
1. De Carlo, Yvonne with Doug Warren. *Yvonne: An Autobiography.* St. Martin's Press. New York. 1987. P. 67
2. Considine, Shaun. *Bette and Joan: The Divine Feud.* E.P. Dutton. New York. 1989. P. 162
3. Proctor, Kay. "Canteen Anecdotes From A Canteen Hostess." *Photoplay.* 1943. P. 84
4. Spada, James. *More Than A Woman: An Intimate Biography of Bette Davis.* Bantam Books. New York. 1993. P. 195
5. Mosley, Roy. *Bette Davis: An Intimate Memoir.* Donald I. Fine, Inc. New York. 1989, 1990. P.116
6. Davis, Bette with Michael Herskowitz. *This 'n' That.* G.P. Putnam's Sons. New York. 1987. P. 128

7. Telegram from Bette Davis to Clarence Offer, Motion Picture Projectionists. Margaret Herrick Library, Academy of Motion Picture Arts and Sciences. Beverly Hills, California
8. Wright, Virginia, *The Los Angeles Daily News.* November 17, 1945
9. "Hollywood's Famed Canteen Mustered Out." *Los Angeles Times.* November 23, 1945. P. A-1
10. *Los Angeles Herald Examiner.* November 23, 1945
11. Ibid.
12. Ashland, Jack. "Invitation To a Wedding of Bette Davis and William Grant Sherry." *Photoplay.* February, 1946. P. 124
13. Davis, Bette. *The Lonely Life: An Autobiography.* New York. G.P. Putnam's Sons. 1962. P. 261
14. Chandler, Charlotte. *The Girl Who Walked Home Alone: Bette Davis: A Personal Biography.* Simon & Schuster Publishers. N.Y. 2006. P. 169

Epilogue
1. Brunson, David. "Voices." *People.* February 9, 1987. P. 55
2. Diane Meredith Volz to authors, July, 2007
3. Not long after the building was demolished, a five-story parking structure was erected on the site.
4. James Washburn to authors, October 30, 2007
5. Davis, Bette. *This 'n' That.* P. 128
6. Endres, Stacey and Robert Cushman. *Hollywood At Your Feet: The Story of the World-Famous Chinese Theatre.* Pomegranate Press, LTD. Los Angeles, London. 1992. P. 224
7. Davis, Bette. *This 'n' That.* P. 117
8. McGrath, Patrick J. *John Garfield: The Illustrated Career in Films and On Stage.* McFarland & Company, Inc. Publishers. Jefferson, North Carolina, and London. 1993. P. 58
9. Davis, Bette. *This 'n' That.* P. 118.
10. Ibid. P. 119
11. Ibid. P.123
12. *Los Angeles Daily News.* October 30, 1943. P. 3
13. Brokaw, Tom. *The Greatest Generation.* Random House, New York. 1998.
14. Ibid. P. 11

SOURCES

Bibliography

Behlmer, Rudy and Tony Thomas. *Hollywood's Hollywood: The Movies About the Movies.* Citadel Press. Seacaucus, N.J. 1975

Brokaw, Tom. *The Greatest Generation.* Random House, New York. 1998

Chandler, Charlotte. *The Girl Who Walked Home Alone: Bette Davis: A Personal Biography.* Simon & Schuster Publishers. N.Y. 2006

Clarke, Gerald. *Get Happy: The Life Of Judy Garland.* Random House. New York. 2000

Considine, Shaun. *Bette and Joan: The Divine Feud.* E.P. Dutton. New York. 1989

Davis, Bette. *The Lonely Life: An Autobiography.* New York. G.P. Putnam's Sons. 1962

Davis, Bette. With Michael Herskowitz. *This 'n' That.* G.P. Putnam's Sons. New York. 1987

De Carlo, Yvonne with Doug Warren. *Yvonne: An Autobiography.* St. Martin's Press. New York. 1987

Endres, Stacey and Robert Cushman. *Hollywood At Your Feet: The Story of the World-Famous Chinese Theatre.* Pomegranate Press, LTD. Los Angeles, London. 1992

Hoopes, Roy. *When The Stars Went To War: Hollywood And World War II.* Random House. New York. 1994

Hunt, Marsha. *The Way We Wore: Styles of the 1930s and 1940s and Our World Since Then.* Fallbrook Publishing, Ltd. Fallbrook, California. 1993

Katz, Ephraim. *The Film Encyclopedia (Second Edition).* Harper Collins, New York, 1994

Kobal, John. *Rita Hayworth: The Time, The Place, The Woman.* W.H. Allen. London, 1977

Lamarr, Hedy. *Ecstacy and Me: My Life as a Woman.* Bartholomew House. 1966

McBride, Joseph. *Searching For John Ford: A Life.* St. Martin's Press. NY 2001

McGee, Tom. *The Girl With the Million Dollar Legs.* Vestal Press. Vestal, New York. 1995

McGrath, Patrick J. *John Garfield: The Illustrated Career in Films and On Stage.* McFarland & Company, Inc. Publishers. Jefferson, North Carolina, and London. 1993

Mosley, Roy. *Bette Davis: An Intimate Memoir.* Donald I. Fine, Inc. New York. 1989

Quirk, Lawrence J. *The Films of Joan Crawford.* The Citadel Press. Seacaucus, New York . 1968

Riva, Maria. *Marlene Dietrich by Her Daughter Maria Riva.* Alfred A. Knopf. New York. 1993

Spada, James. *More Than A Woman: An Intimate Biography of Bette Davis.* Bantam Books. New York. 1993

Starr, Kevin. *Embattled Dreams: California in War and Peace 1940-1950.* Oxford University Press. 2002

Stine, Whitney. *Mother Goddam: The Story of the Career of Bette Davis* With a Running Commentary by Bette Davis. Hawthorn Books. New York, 1974

Tierney, Gene with Mickey Herkowitz. *Self-Portrait.* Wyden Books. 1979/Berkeley Books 1980. New York. Berkeley Edition.

Westmore, Frank and Muriel Davidson. *The Westmores of Hollywood.* J. P. Lippincott Company. Philadelphia. 1976

Wilkerson, Tichi and Marcia Borie. *Hollywood Legends: The Years Of The Hollywood Reporter* Tale Weaver Publishing. Los Angeles, 1988

Wood, Ean. *Dietrich: A Biography.* Sanctuary Publishing, Ltd. London, 2002

Manuscript for unpublished biography of Bette Davis

Manuscript for unpublished biography of Jules Stein

Periodicals

Diary of Jane Lockwood Ferraro
Hollywood Canteen "Chatter"
Hollywood Citizen News
Hollywood Reporter, The
Hollywood Studio Magazine
Liberty Magazine
Los Angeles Daily News
Los Angeles Examiner
Los Angeles Herald Examiner
Los Angeles Times
Milwaukee Journal–Screen–Radio
Movieland
New York Times Magazine
People
Photoplay
Publicity Release, Vic Shapiro And Staff, 1945
Screenland
The Daily News
Warner's Club News

Institutions

Alex Gotleib Archival Research Center, Boston University, Boston, MA

Margaret Herrick Library, Academy of Motion Picture Arts and Sciences, Beverly Hills, CA

Warner Bros. Collection at University of Southern California, Los Angeles, CA

ACKNOWLEDGEMENTS

Stacey Behlmer, Margaret Herrick Library, Academy Of Motion Picture Arts And Sciences

Tracey Boldemann, Hollywood Canteen Foundation

Harry (Dobe) Carey, Jr.

Christina Crawford

Dan Clark–Santa Barbara Digital

Howard Gotlieb Archival Research Center, Boston University

Julie Garfield

Johnny Grant

Barbara Hall, Margaret Herrick Library, Academy Of Motion Picture Arts and Sciences

Patricia King Hanson, American Film Institute

Bob Hope Enterprises

Linda Hope

Grace Houghton

Marsha Hunt

Joseph Jasgur

Howard Johnson

Joan Leslie

A.C. Lyles

Nancy Malone

Nancy Marlowe

Nina Skolsky Marsh

Linda Mehr, Margaret Herrick Library, Academy Of Motion Picture Arts and Sciences

Gerald Oppenheimer, Hollywood Canteen Foundation

Janis Paige

Marvin Paige

Jean Porter

Professional Musicians Local #47

Jane Russell

Meg Smith

Steffi Sidney (Skolsky) Splaver

Gloria Stuart

Roy Thorsen

Christine Clark Torrence

Diane Merideth Volz

Marc Wanamaker–Bison Archives

Warner Bros. Collection, University Of Southern California

James Washburn

Jane Withers

All photographs are from the hollywoodphotographs.com *collection.*

INDEX

Abbott, Bud 34
Abbott and Costello *34*, 110
Above Suspicion (1943) 68
A Guy Named Joe (1943) 176
Air Force (1943) 176
All About Eve (1950) 183
Allen, Gracie 110, *134*
Ambassador Hotel 30
American Legion 178, 184
American Theater Wing 13
Anderson, Corporal Ernest *99*, 102
Anderson, Eddie "Rochester" 36
Andrews Sisters 9, *108*, 109, 163-164
Angel Flight For Veterans 184
Angel, Heather 129
Angels' Table(s) 42, *42*, 111, *137*
"A Night At The Hollywood Canteen" 184
Armed Forces Radio Services (AFRS) 115
Armstrong, Louis *103*, 115
Army Corps Of Engineers 129
Arthur, Jean 16, 36
Ayers, Lew 154
Baldwin, Cay 15
Bambi (1942) 13
Barclay, Don 136
Bari, Lynn 129
Barker, Jess *81*, 134
Barnes, Private Taylor 132
Barney Oldfield's Country Club 129, 131
Baxter, Anne 36
Beds For Buddies 151
Behlmer, Rudy 165
Bell, Sergeant William E. W. *128*, 129, *129*, *130, 131*
Benchley, Robert 65
Bendix, William 74
Bennett, Joan 36
Benny, Jack , 36.115, 163, 165, 179
Bergen, Edgar 110
Bergman, Ingrid 179
Best Years Of Our Lives, The (1946) 181
Beyond The Forest (1946) 19
Blackouts, The Ken Murray's 115
Blair, Janet *49*

Blood and Sand (1941) 94
Body and Soul (1947) 13
Bolger, Ray 110
Bondi, Beulah 11, *57*, 67
"Boogie Woogie Bugle Boy" 87, 109
Boyer, Charles 36, 115
"Boys In The Backroom" 110
Bracken, Eddie 131
Brand, Sybil *142*
Breakfast In Hollywood 153
Breneman, Tom 153
Brian, Mary 132
Bride Came C.O.D., The (1941) 47
British Aviation Aircraft Unit 134
British Grenadier Guardsmen 154
Brodel, Betty 162
Brodel, Joan – see Leslie, Joan 89
Brooks, Leslie *31, 49*
Brokaw, Tom 184
Brown, Joe E. 110, 131, 163
Burke, Billie 179
Burns and Allen 115, 133
Burns, George 110, *134*
Burrett, Lieutenant Howard 132
Cadrez, Florence C. 55
Cagney, James 47, 89, 115
Cameron, Kate 165
Cameron, Rod 131
Canon, Margie 45
Cantor, Eddie 34, 37, *63*, *99*, 110-111, *111*, 115, 131-133, *142*, 176
Carey, Harry (Dobe), Jr. 92
Carey, Harry, Sr. 92
Carlisle, Kitty 163
Carmichael, Hoagy 9, 131
Carroll, Earl 154
Carson, Jack 110, 163, 179
Cassini, Oleg 135
Cavallero, Carmen 115, 163
Chapman, Marguerite *50*
"Chatanooga Choo Choo" 13, 87
"Chatter" 43, 45
Ciro's *14*, 16, 17, 109
Civies (Baseball Team) 131

Clark, Captain Albert L. 133
Clark, Dane *161*, 162
Coburn, Charles 133
Cocoanut Grove, The 109
Colbert, Claudette *69*, 113, 115
Cole, Woody 56-57
Coleman, Ronald 16, 74, *141*, *179*
Colonna, Jerry 179
Columbia Studios 16
Cooper, Gary 9, 36, 89, 115
Cornell, Katherine 159
Costello, Lou 34, 74
Cowan, Sergeant DeForest 45
Crawford, Christina 68, 74
Crawford, Joan 36, *65*, 67-68, 162-163
Creative Enterprises, Inc. 181
Cregar, Laird 40
Crosby, Bing 9, 36, 68, 133, 159
Crosby Quartet 9
Cry Havoc (1943) 176
"Dance With A Dolly" 87
Dantine, Helmut 163
Darnell, Linda 65, *73*, *95*, 133, *140*
Daves, Delmer 159-160, 182
Davis, Bette
  against racism 17, 100-102
  All About Eve (1950) 183
  Beyond The Forest (1946) 19
  Bride Came C.O.D., The (1941) 47
  and Canteen closing 177-179
  and Canteen opening 34, *35*, 36
  as co-founder 9, 15, *17*, 19, *19*, 29, 34, *35*, *51*, 55, *124*, 131, 132, 133, *136*
  and Distinguished Civilian Service Medal 183-184, *183*
  enlists Chef Joseph Milani 41
  enlists Jules Stein 15
  and finding a building 19
  and first conceptual meeting 13
  and Grauman's Chinese Theater honor 183
  as guiding force 9, 57, 66, 92, *99*, 175-176
  Hollywood Canteen (1944) *160*, 162-163
  and Hollywood Guild and Canteen 155
  and Hollywood Victory Committee 29, 45, 47

In This Is Our Life (1942) 99
Jezebel (1938) 66
Jimmy The Gent (1934) 47
Letter, The (1940) 66
and "Chatter" 43
Mr. Skeffington (1944) 163
and new Hollywood Canteen (1951) 182
Now, Voyager (1942) 13
as performer at the Hollywood Canteen 66, 115, 136, *148*
as president of the Hollywood Canteen 66, *77*, *116*, 131, 132, *139*, *143*, *145*, 177, 178, 179, 181, 183
and Stage Door Canteen *24*
Thank Your Lucky Stars (1943) 159
and *The Talk Of The Town* premiere party at Ciro's 16, *17*
DeCarlo, Yvonne 175
Dee, Frances 74
de Havilland, Olivia 37, 88, 111, *123*, 132-133
DeMille, Cecil B. 152, 159
Destination Tokyo (1943) 160, 176
Dietrich, Marlene 9, *29*, 36, 37, 45, 67, *67*, *81*, *90*, 92, *96*, *106*, 110, *128*, 129, 132, *145*, 159, 177
Disney, Walt 13,
Dmytryk, Edward 181
Dolin, Anton 117
Donald Gets Drafted (1942) 13
"Don't Fence Me In" 109, *162*, 164, 165
"Don't Get Around Much Anymore" 109
Dorsey, Jimmy 115, 163
Dorsey, Tommy , *80*, 115
Doughgirls, The (1944*)* 162
Drunkard, The 19
Draftees (Baseball Team) 131
Dunne, Irene 30, *36*, 37, *39*, *53*, 65, *163*, 176
Durbin, Deanna 37, *97*, 109, *126*, *128*, 129, *131*, 176
Durante, Jimmy *130*
Ecstasy And Me 66
Eddy, Nelson 117
Edwards, Florida 87-88
Eighth Air Force 132
El Capitan Theater (Vine St.) 115
Ellington, Duke 36, *105*, 115
Emerson, Faye *156*, 163, 176
Ernie Pyle Post No. 626, 178
Executive Order 9981, 99
Farnum, Dustin 152
Faulkner, Chuck 131
FBI 15, *54*, 56
Field, Virginia *14*
Florentine Gardens 110, 154, 182, *182*
Flynn, Errol 153
Follow The Boys (1944) 159

Fonda, Henry 179
Fontanne, Lynn 159
Ford, John 41, 92, 113
Ford, Captain K. M. 133
Ford, Mary 15, 41, 92, *142*, 155, 182
Four Daughters (1938) 13
Fox, Colonel William J. 133
Francen, Victor 163
Francis, Guy 181
French Merchant Marines 154
Fridner, Julienne *56*
Francis, Kay 71
Gabin, Jean *29*, 37, 67
Gable, Clark, Captain 132
Garden of Allah Hotel 153
Garfield, John
against racism 17, 100, 102,
Air Force (1943) 176
and 4-F status 13
Body and Soul (1947) 13
as co-founder 9, 15, 19, *19*, 29, 34, 45, 65, 75, 131, 132, 133, *136*, *171*, 183
Destination Tokyo (1943) 176
and finding a building 19
and first conceptual meeting 13
Four Daughters (1938) 13
Hollywood Canteen (1944) 162-163
Humoresque (1946) 13
And Canteen opening 34, 37
Postman Always Rings Twice, The (1946) 13
and Stage Door Canteen 13, 45
and *The Talk Of The Town* premiere party at Ciro's 16
Garland, Judy 37, 109, 117, *171*
Garson, Greer 91
Gaynor, Janet 155
"Getting Corns For My Country" 164
"Gettysburg Address, The" 112
Giant (1956) 113
Gilda (1946) 94
Gleason, James 179
Goddard, Paulette *59*, *84*, 133
Going My Way (1944) 165
Golden Spike Theater, The 181
Goodman, Benny 17, 115
Gordon, Mary 67, *77*, 163
Gottlieb, Alex 162
Grable, Betty 11, 37, 74, 92, 94, 133, 134, *143*
Grady, Billy 45
Granlund, Nils Thor (NTG) 110, *117*
Grant, Cary 16, 37, *70*, *83*, 111, 115
Granville, Bonita *25*, *56*, 74, 179
Greatest Story Ever Told, The (1965) 113
Greenstreet, Sydney *161*, 163
Groen, John te 182
Hale, Alan 163, 176

Haley, Jack 179
Hall Of Honor 132, *145*, 170
Hamilton, Gerald 73
Hayes, Helen 159
Haynes, Sergeant Bill 132
Hayward, Susan 37
Hayworth, Rita 11, *28*, 37, 67, *86*, 92, 111, *173*
Heidt, Horace 115
Hendreid, Paul 13, 65, 163
Herald Examiner 179
"He's My Guy" 36
Hitler, Adolph 176
Hollister, Carroll 15
Hollywood Canteen (1944) 68, 91, 129, 135, *158*, 158-165, *159*, *160*, *161*, *162*, 179, 182,
Hollywood Canteen, attendance of servicemen 37, 41, 58, 129, 133, 179
Hollywood Canteen, building demolition 181
Hollywood Canteen, building remodeling 19
Hollywood Canteen, Christmas 99, 133, *140*, *141*, *142*, *143*
Hollywood Canteen, closing. 177-179
Hollywood Canteen, First Birthday *124*, 131, *132*, 133, *133*, *136*, *137*, *138*, *171*
Hollywood Canteen, food 15, 41, 42
Hollywood Canteen Foundation 178, 179, 182, *182*, 184
Hollywood Canteen, fundraiser at Ciro's 17, *17*, 164
Hollywood Canteen, hours 15, 16, 58, 117, 179
Hollywood Canteen, hostesses 16, 30, 55-56, *56*, 57, *73*, 88, 89, 101-102, *105*, 175
Hollywood Canteen, layout – See Appendix 185
Hollywood Canteen, misuse of name 181
Hollywood Canteen, opening 32-37, *38*. 39
Hollywood Canteen, rules 57-58
Hollywood Canteen, Thanksgiving 133, *139*, 178, 179
Hollywood Canteen, volunteers, number of 15, 16, 55, 57
Hollywood Guild and Canteen *150*, *151*, 150-155
Hollywoodland Sign 164, 181
Hollywood Reporter, The 16, 155
Hollywood Victory Committee 29, 45, 47
"Honeysuckle Rose" 109
Hope, Bob 9, 11, 110, *114*, 115, *116*, 132, 134, *134*, *145*, 159, *164*, 179, 184
Hopper, Hedda *76*, 111, *154*, 155
Horne, Lena 109, *112*, 133
Hume, Benita *141*
Humoresque (1944) 13
Hunt, Marsha 37, *56*, 71, *73*, 74, 111, 129, 176
Hussey, Ruth 129

INDEX

Hutton, Betty 9, 37, 109, 115, 159, *160*, 162, 176
Hutton, Robert *159, 161*
"Ida, Sweet As Apple Cider" 111
"I Had The Craziest Dream Last Night" 175
Ingram, Rex 17
In This Our Life (1942) 99, 102
Iturbi, Jose 117, *125*, 133
James, Claire *73*
James, Harry 94, 115, 134
Jessell, George 111
Jezebel (1938) 66
Jimmy The Gent (1934) 47
Johnson, Howard 94
Johnson, Johnny 131
Jones, Spike 115
Jules Stein Eye Institute 184
Kaye, Danny 110, *120*
Kay Kyser's Kollege of Musical Knowledge 115
Keaton, Buster 65, 131, *168*
Kenyon, Doris *142*
Keyes, Evelyn *50*, 56
King, Walter Wolff 131
Kismet (1944) 92
Klemperer, Otto 117
Kobal, John 94,
Korean War 182, *182*
Koverman, Ida 134
Krupa, Gene 115
Kyser, Kay 36, *61*, 87, *105,* 112, 115, 132, *134,* 179
Lake Norconian Naval Hospital 71,
Lake, Veronica 37
Lamarr, Hedy 37, 66, *89*, 91, 92, *107*, 115, 134, *163*, 179
Lamour, Dorothy 133
Landers, Captain Jack 132
Langford, Frances 109, 132
LaPlant, Lucille 179
LaRue, Jack *105, 139*
Lasky, Jesse, 160, 162
Lassie Come Home (1943) 67
Laughton, Charles 112, 117
Laura (1944) 135
Lawrence, Gertrude 117
Leave Her To Heaven (1945) 135
Lee, Thomas 181
Le Grand Comedy Theater 181
Lehr, Mrs. Abraham, see Lehr, Anne Neill,
Lehr, Anne Neill (Mom Lehr) 151-155, *151*
LeRoy, Mervin 15, 37, 132, *134*, 155, 182
Leslie, Joan 9, 37, 74, 89, 91, 129, *131*, 132, *146*, 162, 165, 179
Lesser, Sol 159-160, 182

Letter, The (1940) 66
Lewin, Jean 15, 43
Lewis, Ted 110, *119*
Liberty magazine 152, 153
"Lili Marlene" 110
Loder, John 134
Lorre, Peter 163
Los Angeles Times 102, 133, *174*
Louise, Anita *25*, 74
Love Affair (1939) 160
Loy, Myrna 155
Lunt, Alfred 159
Lupino, Ida 163
Lyles, A. C. , 109
MacDonald, Jeanette *43*, 74, 109, 117
MacMurray, Fred 37, 74
Madame Currie (1943) 132
"Ma, He's Making Eyes At Me" 111
Main, Majorie 155
"Makin' Whoopee" 111
Manning, Irene *70, 147,* 163
March Field 57
Markova, Alicia 117
Marshall, Herbert 65, *141*
Martin, Freddy 115, 131
Masoner, Lieutenant (J.G.) William 133
Mature, Victor, Chief Petty Officer 132
Mayer, Louis B. 134-135
McBride, Joseph 102
McCracken, Joan 110, 163
McDowell, Roddy 67, 74, 92, *153*, 179
McKenzie, Faye 56, *91*, 110
Menken, Helen 45
Meredith, Diane 87, 102, 181
Milani, Chef Joseph Leopold 41, *41*, 129, 132, 182
Mildred Pierce (1945) 68
Millar, Mack 33, 182
Miller, Ann 74, 110, 133, *140*
Miller, Glenn 56
Millionth Man 129, *129*, 130, 131, 162
Mocambo 109
"Moonlight Becomes You" 175
"Moonlight Serenade" 87
Moran, Dolores 163
Morehead, Baron 182
Morgan, Dennis 109, 163
Morocco (1930) 92
Morris, Mason 182
Morrison, Patricia 109. 129, 132
Mother Goddam 42, 115
Motion Picture Illustrators Guild 20, *21*
Motion Picture Painters and Scenic Artists, Local #644 18
Mr. Skeffington (1944) 163
Mrs. Miniver (1942) 132,

Murder In The Red Barn 19
Murder, He Says (1945) 109, 176
Murray, Ken 110, 115, *123*
Muse, Clarence 102
Music Corporation of America (MCA) 15, 55, 155
Musicians Union (American Federation of Musicians, Local #47 & #767) 115
Mussolini, Benito 176
Myers, Carmel 135-136
National Association For The Advancement Of Colored People (NAACP) 99
Nave, Sergeant Bert R. 183
Nesbit, Meg 56-57
New York Daily News 165
Nicholas Brothers 110
99th Pursuit Squadron 99
92nd Infantry Division 99
Now, Voyager (1942) 13
Oberon, Merle *76*, 88
O'Brien, Pat 37, 74
O'Connor, Una *161*
O'Driscoll, Martha *25*, 56, *144*
Office Of Price Administration (OPA) 41
Osborne, Robert 182
Our Town (1940) 159
Paddock Club, The 131
Paige, Janis 134, 162, 179, 181
Pajama Game, The 135
Paralyzed Veterans Of America 184
Pardon My Sarong (1942) 162
Parker, Eleanor 163
Parsons, Louella *62,* 111, 155
Pearl Harbor 11, 29, 73, 152, 177
People magazine 181
Peterson, Lawrence, Boatswain's First Mate 133
Pickford, Mary *124*, 132, 155
Pidgeon, Walter 111
Pilla, Henry , *87*
Porter, Cole 160
Porter, Jean 56, 71, 115, 129
Postman Always Rings Twice, The (1946) 13
Powell, Eleanor 37
Powell, Jane 109, *178*
Prinz, LeRoy 164
Proctor, Kay 175-176
Quiz Kids, The 111
Rafferty, Frances 56
Raft, George 111
Rakowski, Seaman William 129
Rathbone, Basil 42, *47, 52,* 74, 117
Rathbone, Ouida 42, *52*
Reagan, Captain Ronald 132, *133*
Red Barn, The 19-20, *20*
Reed, Donna 56

Reif, Harry *141*
Reynolds, Marjorie *167*
Rhapsody In Blue (1945) 89
Rice, Yeoman Seymour. *26, 31*
Rito, Ted Fio 115
Ritz, Jimmy *14*
Riva, Maria 92
Robinson, Bill "Bogangles" *60*, 110
Robinson, Edward G. 37, 179
Rogers, Ginger *172*
Rogers, Roy 109, 163, 164, 165
Rooney, Mickey 37, *41, 72, 101, 110,* 111, 136
Roosevelt, President Franklin Delano 11, 41
Rubinstein, Arthur 117
Rudy Vallee's Coast Guard Band 36, *113*
"Rum And Coca Cola" 115
Russell, Jane 37, *152*
Russell, Rosalind 111
Sakall, S. Z. , *122*, 163
Schoor, Pvt. Bernard W. , 43
Schwab's Pharmacy 153
Scott, Randolph 37
Scott, Zackary 163
Screen Actors Guild (SAG) 29, 45, 102, 160, 161
Screen Cartoonists Guild 20
Screen Office Employees Guild 136
Screen Set Designers Guild 19
Segregation of Armed Services *98*, 99
Selznick, David O. 16
Sergeant York (1941) 89, 160
Shanghai Express (1932) 92
Shannon, Colonel Harold D. 34
Sheridan, Ann 37, *154,* 162
She Wore A Yellow Ribbon (1949) 113
Shipp, Cameron 182
Shirley, Anne 56
Shore, Dinah 37, *78,* 109, 115, *164,* 179
Shubert, Lee 13
Silvers, Phil 110
Simms, Ginny *32,* 36, 58, 109, 129, 132
Simpson, Charles "Mickey" *110,* 113, 131
Sinatra, Frank *69,* 109, 115
Skelton, Red 37, 65, 110, 111, 115, 117, *121,* 157
Skolsky, Sidney 67
Smith, Alexis 163
Smith, Kate *74*
Smith, Stuff 17
Sons Of The Pioneers 163
Southern, Ann *62,* 176
"Souvenir" 163
Special Operations Warrior Foundation 184
Spencer, Staff Sergeant Jack 183
Squaw Man, The (1914) 152
Stagecoach (1939) 113

Stage Door Canteen (1944) 159-160, 179
Stage Door Canteen, The *24,* 45, 159-160
Stanwyck, Barbara 163
"Stardust" 87
Stark, Juanita *14*
Starr, Kevin 100
Star-Spangled Rhythm (1942) 159
"Star Spangled Banner, The" 101, 131, 179
Stein, Doris *25,* 55
Stein, Jules 15, *19,* 29, 30, 55, 155, 160, 182, 184
Steiner, Max 13
Stevens, Craig 163
Stevens, K. T. *131*
Stevens, Toni *152*
Stewart, Lieutenant James 132, 179
Stoke McGraw's Shell Gas Station 33
Stokowski, Leopold 115, 117, 132, *136, 138*
"Stormy Weather" 109
Stuart, Gloria 92
Sunset Boulevard (1950) 153
Suspense 13
"Sweet Dreams, Sweetheart" 163, 165
"Swinging On A Star" 165
Szigeti, Joseph 163, 165
Tag Dance 88, *93*
Talk Of The Town, The (1942) *16,* 16, 17, 100
Taplinger, Bob 16
Taylor, Robert 37, 132 (as Lietenant Commander)
Ten Commandments, The (1956) 164
Thank Your Lucky Stars (1943) 159
"The Bee" 163
The Daily News 179
"The Lord's Prayer" 117, 131
"They're Either Too Young Or Too Old" 159
This 'n' That 183
Thomas, John Charles 117, 131
Thomas, Tony 165
Thompson, Corporal Keith 132
Thorson, Roy 184
Thousands Cheer (1943) 159
3:10 To Yuma (1957) 160
Tierney, Gene 37, 135
Till The End Of Time (1946) 181
Tilton, Martha 58, 109, *152*
Titanic (1997) 92
Tjaden, Donna May 134 (also see Paige, Janis)
Tracy, Spencer 37, 45, 65, *66, 79,* 111, 133, *139,* 176
Trevor, Claire 74, *93*
Trigger 163
Truman, President Harry S. 99, 177
"Tumbling Tumbleweeds" 163
Turner Classic Movies 182
Turner, Lana 37, 111, 115, *128,* 129, *131*

USO 182, 184
Vallee, Rudy 36, *166*
Variety 165
V-E Day 176
Veloz and Yolanda *82,* 110
V-J Day *174, 175,* 177
Volunteers' parties 129, 131
WACS (Women's Army Corp.) 58
Wallace, Beryl 154
Wallace, Vice President Henry 65, *164*
Wallace, J.K. Spike 15
Warner Bros. 9, 13, 68, 89, 91, 99, 129, 135, 159, 160, 161, 163, 164, 179
Warner, Jack 176
Washburn, James 102, 183
Wasserman, Lew 15
Waterloo Bridge (1940) 132,
Waters, Bunny 87, *170*
WAVES (Women Accepted For Volunteer Service) 58
Welles, Orson 111, *118,* 153, 159
Westmore, Perc 136, *148*
"What Are You Doing The Rest Of Your Life?" 163
Whorf, Richard 20
Wilder, Billy 153
Wilkerson, W. R. "Billy" 16, 155
Williams, Chili *122*
Willis, Superior Judge Henry M. 87
Wilson, Carey 15
Wilson, Marie 110, 115
Withers, Jane *42,* 87
Woolley, Monty 154
Wright, Cobina *142*
Wright, Virginia 179
Wyler, Major William 132, 181
Wyman, Jane *14,* 37, 132, *133,* 162, 163
Yankee Doodle Dandy (1942) 89, 164
Ybarra, Alfred 15, 16, 19, *19, 170,* 182
"You'd Be So Nice To Come Home To" 87
Young, Loretta *23,* 37, *55*
You Were Never Lovelier (1942) 94
Zdiriencik, Private John 132

To help present day servicemen and women, donations may be made to:

**THE HOLLYWOOD CANTEEN FOUNDATION
PO BOX 30
BEVERLY HILLS, CA 90213**

Bear Manor Media

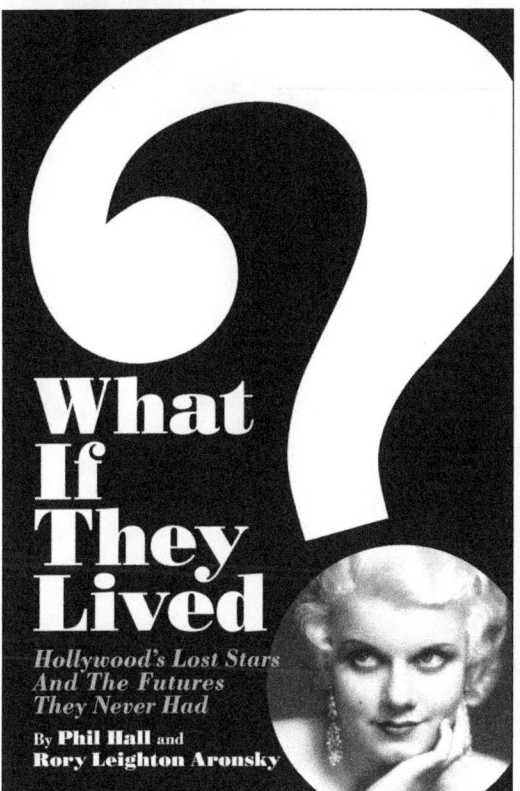

Classic Cinema.
Timeless TV.
Retro Radio.
WWW.BEARMANORMEDIA.COM

CPSIA information can be obtained
at www.ICGtesting.com
Printed in the USA
LVHW061550260821
696189LV00003B/238